BRAD PITT
THE RISE TO STARDOM

BRAD PITT

THE RISE TO STARDOM

BRIAN J. ROBB

Plexus, London

Copyright © 1996 by Brian J. Robb
Published by Plexus Publishing Limited
55a Clapham Common Southside
London SW4 9BX
First Printing 1996

British Library Cataloguing in Publication Data
Robb, Brian J.
Brad Pitt: the rise to stardom
1.Pitt, Brad 2. Motion picture actors and actresses -
United States - Biography
I. Title
791.43028092

ISBN 0 85965 241 6

Printed in Great Britain by Hillman Printers (Frome) Ltd
Designed by Phil Smee

10 9 8 7 6 5 4 3 2 1

Acknowledgements

My love and thanks to my wife Brigid and son Cameron for
their patience with my working hours and constant
support.

Special thanks are due to the dynamic duo George
Fergus and John Lavaille; John Riley at BFI Information
and Library Services and Mike Wingate at C&A video.

Organisations and individuals whose assistance was
invaluable include The Directors Guild of America and
The American Film Institute. Also gratitude to everyone at
Plexus and at The Central Times, as well as everyone at
the various film production, distribution and publicists
offices.

I'd like to thank the following magazines and newspapers for their coverage of Brad Pitt over the years:

TV Hits/ Liz Simon; *Film Review*; *Sky Magazine*;
Entertainment Weekly; *People Weekly*; *Company*;
Live & Kicking; *Nineteen*; *Options*; *Big!*; *Mizz*; *My
Guy*; *New Musical Express*; *New Woman*; *OK!*;
Prima; *Smash Hits*; *Cinescape*; *Bliss*; *Gay Times*;
Screen International; *Vanity Fair*; *National
Enquirer*; *Select*; *Maxim*; *Cosmopolitan*; *The List*;
Sci-Fi Entertainment; *Time Out*; *The Face*; *Rolling
Stone*; *Monthly Film Bulletin*; *Time*; *Variety*; *New
Yorker*; *New Statesman & Society*; *Film Monthly*;
The Guardian; *Daily Record*; *Mail on Sunday*;
Daily Mail; *Sunday Telegraph*; *The Independent*;
The Evening Standard; *Daily Telegraph*;
Edinburgh Evening News; *Sunday Express*;
Spectator; *Today*; *The Hampstead and Highgate
Express*; *The New York Times*; *The Observer*; *The
Irish Times*; *The Belfast Telegraph*; *The Financial
Times*; *The Morning Star*; *The Sunday Post*; *The
People*, *The Daily Express*, and *The Los Angeles
Times*.

Also thanks are due to the staff of BFI Stills,
Posters and Designs and the following libraries and
film companies for supplying photographs:
Jon Ragel/ Onyx/ Retna; All Action; Michael
Putland/Retna; La Moine/ Katz; John Paschal/
Celebrity Photo; C. Delmas/ Sygma; Ian McKell/
Retna; Levi's; Mark Anderson/ Retna; George Holz/
Retna; Steve Granitz/ Retna; MGM; The Ronald
Grant Film Archive; The British Film Institute;
Richard Corman/ Onyx/ Retna; Morgan Creek
International; Jean Cummings/ All Action; Tri-Star
Pictures; Rob Brown/ Retna; Geffen Pictures; People
in Pictures; Warner Brothers; Entertainment; Doug
Peters/ All Action; New Line Productions Inc/ New
Line Cinema/ Peter Sorel; PolyGram Filmed
Entertainment; Dave Hogan/ All Action; Bill Davilla/
Retna; Sam Levi/ Retna; Mojgan B. Azimi/ Retna;
Brad Fierce/ Snap/ Katz; Michael Benabib/ Retna;
Laura Luongo/ People in Pictures
Film stills courtesey of: Guild Film; Columbia Tri-
Star; PolyGram Filmed Entertainment; Rank Film
Distributors Limited; Paramount Pictures;
Entertainment; New Line Productions Inc/ New Line
Cinema; Warner Brothers Entertainment; MGM;
Pathe Entertainment/ United International Pictures;
Morgan Creek International; Geffen Pictures; Nelson
Entertainment; Shuler-Donner Productions;
Miramax; Vega Film Productions; Allied Filmmakers;
Viacom Pictures; Propaganda Films

Contents

1 The Missouri Kid

IN THE HOLLYWOOD of the 1990s Brad Pitt is one of the biggest stars, and he seems to have reached this enviable position with almost next to no effort. His rise has been unstoppable, from his first 15 minutes of fame as a sensual robber in 1991's controversial hit movie *Thelma and Louise*. In 1995 he won great acclaim for his role as a cop on the trail of a satanic serial killer in the surprise box office smash *Seven*. An Oscar nomination followed for his supporting role in the sci-fi thriller *Twelve Monkeys*. From the boy in a Levi jeans TV advert to a pay packet of $10 million a movie in the space of just under a decade is no mean feat for any aspiring actor.

Brad Pitt, however, is not just any actor. He's been blessed with the kind of good looks and easy charm that guarantee a huge fan following, regardless of true acting talent. The advantage that Pitt has over most other TV-to-movies teen idols is that he can actually turn in a more than worthy performance, as his dramatic turns in Robert Redford's *A River Runs Through It* and his challenging work alongside Bruce Willis in Terry Gilliam's *Twelve Monkeys* and Robert DeNiro in *Sleepers* show.

Bill and Jane Pitt's first born son, William Bradley Pitt, came into the world in the small town of Shawnee, Oklahoma on 18th December 1963. For his mother Jane, working as a school counsellor, the health and well-being of her new son was uppermost in her mind. For his father, William Senior, known as Bill, the arrival of his son was a welcome break from the routine of his life as a trucker. However, he knew that his work meant that he wouldn't be seeing as much of 'little Brad', as the new child was known to distinguish him from his father, as he might like to.

One of Pitt's college friends felt he could see Pitt's parents in his own make-up. 'Brad looks like his father and has the personality of his mother,' Chris Schudy told *Rolling Stone* in a 1994 profile. 'His mother is so down to earth, just a super woman. His dad is a great guy, but more reserved. *A River Runs Through It* is almost a mirror of Brad's family. When I saw the movie, I called him and said "You're not even acting, it's just your home unit."'

The home unit was on the move soon after Brad's birth. Bill Pitt was offered a better-paid trucking job based in Springfield, a larger metropolis than the small town of Shawnee. Pitt's new home town was located in the shadow of the Ozark Mountains, which cross the borders of Missouri and Arkansas.

Relocating to Springfield was the first and last move for the new family. Pitt's parents and his brother Douglas, born when Brad was three years old, and sister Julie, born two years after Douglas, still live happily in the town while the elder Pitt pursues his career in Hollywood.

The young Pitt doesn't seem to have suffered from his father's absence for long periods of time due to work. Bill Pitt made sure he spent plenty of time with his children when he was at home, and whenever possible he'd try and take the kids on the road with him. These journeys were the nearest thing to real holidays that the family enjoyed.

Sister Julie describes the family as happy and close-knit: 'I always looked up to both of my brothers. I just thought they were the greatest. Doug and Brad really played off each other. We just had such a close family, and I think that gave us confidence. I think that's what allowed Brad to become an actor. Sometimes I can't believe that this guy from Springfield made it, but Brad has always succeeded in what he's done, and he's always had a way with people.' Now with a young family of her own, Julie maintains those close ties with her parents and brothers.

Brother Doug, who now runs his own computer company in Springfield, reinforces the impression of a well-balanced, loving family. 'He's a regular Joe,' he says of his $10 million per picture superstar brother. It's Brad Pitt's stubborn streak, his willingness to work against the flow that Doug reckons has allowed him to succeed in the shark-infested waters of modern Hollywood. 'If the rush was for everyone to go out and buy Harleys, Brad wouldn't buy one.'

'Brad has always done things his own way or not at all. When he was told to walk on the right, he would walk on the left. But he's so good at things and so charming he has always got away with it. Whenever I tried to imitate him, I always got into trouble.'

Pitt would later call his parents 'the biggest guides in my life,' laying any blame or credit for his acting success on his mother. It was Jane who encouraged her son to express himself and who began to suspect he might have some acting talent. 'She just thought it from day one,' said Pitt.

It wasn't only family members who recognised the talents brewing in Brad. As a six-year-old choir boy, Pitt came to the attention of piano accompanist Connie Bilyeu at South Haven Baptist Church. 'You couldn't keep from watching Brad because his face was so expressive,' she told *People* magazine. She was so impressed with Pitt's scene stealing at the choir that she later became his high school drama coach. 'He would move his little mouth so big with all the words that he would attract everyone's attention.'

Family life for the Pitts seems to have been quite idyllic. The family weren't well off, but neither were they particularly poor. Springfield, Missouri was a typical middle-income, mid-Western town. There was no trauma from a parents divorce to fuel Brad Pitt's acting ambitions. There was no peripatetic childhood, with the family crossing the States in search of happiness. There was no childhood insecurity or parental abuse to be poured out later into press interviews. In fact, although they enjoyed only a modest standard of living there was no real lack whatsoever in Brad Pitt's early life. His parents worked hard to provide for the family. 'I understand that people work – my father spent 36 years, six days a week on the job,' Pitt later told *Vanity Fair*.

His parents, for all their Baptist-inspired discipline and strictness, provided Brad with an emotional stability and moral guidance that allowed him to grow up in a safe, secure and carefree environment. Although tough on him about following their religion and about attending church, Bill and Jane were not typically restrictive Baptist parents in most other ways.

According to Pitt, one incident with his father during his early teen years illustrates his parents' enlightened approach to discipline and child-rearing. Losing his juvenile temper during a heated game of tennis, Pitt ended up screaming and shouting and throwing his racket to the ground in an out-of-control tantrum. Approaching his son between games, Bill Pitt asked him a simple question. 'He just said "Are you having fun?" I got all huffy and said "no". He looked at me and said, "Then don't do it," and then walked away. Boy, that put me in my place. I should have gotten my ass kicked, but he was so above that.'

Although young Pitt saw benefits in his parents' Baptist religion and its effects on him - 'it kept my mind on bigger things' - he was like any other child who had to sit through church services: easily bored and in search of a distraction. His rebellion took the childish form of wanting to disrupt the service by making a loud noise and drawing attention to himself – always good skills for any would-be actor to develop at an early age. 'I wanted to stand up and yell.'

Kickapoo High School was another source of stability in Pitt's early life, along with his family and their religion. The school allowed him to discover the academic subjects, including writing and sciences, that interested him and at which he excelled. He also took the opportunity to get involved in non-academic activities, from student government to madrigal singing, an interest developed from his choir days. But even in his school days, Pitt seems to have been unusually aware of his physical attractiveness, and he won an entry in his yearbook, *The Kickapoo Gold*, as 'Best Dressed Student'.

It wasn't all sweetness and light, though, at school, when a scuffle with another pupil turned into a physical fight with one of his teachers. 'The teacher got involved,' Pitt told *Movieline* magazine, 'and she got her dress ripped. It was over something stupid - I can't even remember. I'm the one who hit the teacher. I know I didn't win, but I didn't get my ass kicked.'

School friend Greg Pontious witnessed the incident: 'He wouldn't back down once he confronted a situation. One

Brad in his freshman year at college. The future still looks unexceptional.

day in class somebody spouted off at him and he went after the guy. A teacher got in the middle of the fight and was punched in the face. It was a bloody fight that shocked everyone. No one thought he had it in him to hurt someone badly. It nearly got him thrown out of school.'

Pam Senter, another friend who'd known Pitt since they were both aged five, remembered a different side to Pitt's school days. 'Brad and I went on church trips together and he was always fun to be with – constantly entertaining. He and his friends sang at assembly. They called themselves The Brief Boys. It was ridiculous. They wore their underwear and sang Beach Boys songs with made up lyrics. I think it was Brad's idea – he showed off his body anytime he could. He never talked about wanting to be an actor but now I look back on it, he was an entertainer all along.' It was another example of the young Pitt being conscious of his looks and using them to his advantage.

Like the well rounded, all-American student he was, Pitt was inevitably involved in baseball. Although he didn't excel at the sport, his experiences on the field of play did scar him for life – literally. 'This one is from baseball,' Pitt told *Rolling Stone* writer Chris Mundy, pointing to a cheekbone scar, 'a pop fly that I lost in the sun. I still threw the guy out on the second after it dropped on my face.'

School plays were his real passion, although at this early stage in his acting career he hardly swept audiences off their feet, gaining only supporting parts. It seems that he never pushed himself forward for the leading parts in the school productions, as if he didn't yet have the confidence to emerge from the wings to claim the spotlight for himself. But they did give him the chance to turn his hand to drama and comedy, and even musicals.

Movies were a constant in Pitt's teenage years, and he can remember to this day the films of the late 1970s that made an impact on him. He enjoyed *Saturday Night Fever* on its first release in 1977. It wasn't the obvious attraction, though,

that made Pitt remember the movie. 'Not because of the dancing, but because they got the street life. It was a whole 'nother world than I'd been living in, but I knew it was right, I knew it was true,' he recalled. Robert Redford's 1980 Oscar-winning domestic drama *Ordinary People* also stuck amongst his movie memories. Timothy Hutton's Best Supporting Actor turn as the son treading warily through his teenage years must have struck a chord with Pitt. It may also have started him thinking about the acting business a bit more seriously.

The earliest movie Pitt could recall seeing also featured Redford, in *Butch Cassidy and the Sundance Kid* (1969), released when he was six, but it was 1968's *Planet of the Apes* that really impressed him. Seeing the film on late 70s re-release on a family trip to the drive-in, Pitt was perched on the hood of the family car, clutching a Kool-Aid and a tub of popcorn. He was transported to another world, a planet ruled by apes that in the film's shock

Brad with his classmates.

conclusion turns out to be a future Earth. Pitt read into the meaning of the film lessons he was learning from his family's own Baptist religion: 'I think it's actually very accurate to religion in general today. Don't shake the herd.'

Pitt recalled other films that had made an impact on his impressionable young mind. 'I think of the 70s movies, the ones I grew up with. I remember *Dog Day Afternoon*. I remember [*One Flew Over the*] *Cuckoo's Nest* very heavily. I remember *Butch and Sundance*. I remember a movie on television called *The Jericho Mile*: this guy in prison who just ran, and it turned out he could be competing with the fastest men in the world, but that wasn't why he did it...'

These trips to the cinema were important to the teenager. Even if he wasn't consciously planning a career for himself up on the silver screen, he was learning something about the movies, simply by watching them. He saw many movies, but he does seem to recall those that have lasted the test of time and come to be regarded as modern cinema classics. It's as if the actor-to-be had already cultivated

Brad at a high school prom with his current girlfriend.

a built-in ability to judge good quality material when it crossed his path.

Movies weren't Brad Pitt's only teenage passion – naturally music was a big part of his life too. He'd bought The Who concept album of *Tommy* before he went out to see the film, sitting through it twice to see the pinball wizard section again. The record itself hadn't come easy: 'I had to save up double, 'cause it was a double album.' Having heard the Elton John song 'Daniel', he popped out to buy the *Captain Fantastic* album. Like many teenagers he toyed with being a rock star, strumming a guitar in his bedroom in Springfield.

Pitt had always been popular at school and attracted girls around him from a very early age. His growing sense of the dramatic mixed with his budding romantic side early in his teenage years when he wrote the message 'Hi, Sara' in the snow, next to a giant carved snow heart, as a very public love note to his first serious girlfriend, Sara Hart. She shared his interests in movies and music, accompanying him on weekend trips to the cinema and concerts. The relationship was so strong that many of Pitt's school contemporaries and even his own parents felt they were destined to get married.

Sara may have been Pitt's longest-lasting school days girlfriend, but she was not his first. In Junior High a girl named Kim Bell had won the hard-fought right to be his girl when he was aged 14. Later, as the married Kim Hubbard, she recalled their school days. 'He was a lovely guy. Now my daughter has his pictures all over her bedroom wall.'

Pitt recalled his first encounter with naked women for *Premiere* magazine. 'Somewhere in early elementary school we found a house that was being built, and we found a stack of the old *Playboy*s at the site. Well, I was very impressed. I was just so overwhelmed.' An anonymous friend recalled this epiphany in a British Sunday newspaper supplement profile. 'Brad has been obsessed with women since he was little. The first time he saw pictures of naked women, he went mad. From then on, he was determined to have a girlfriend as soon as possible.'

With the images came the school playground slang and the insistent questions to parents and to those older kids in school who always seemed to be in the know. 'Two kids up the street kept using the word "fuck", and I asked mom what it was, and that's how we got into the whole sex talk. She told me "We don't use that word, this word is slang, but we do use the phrase 'sexual intercourse,' and here it is." With the diagrams. I remember vividly, at that time, being horrified.'

Pitt's youthful horror at the whole idea of sex was short lived, and by the seventh grade his good looks and easy charm had resulted in his basement becoming the venue for the school's frequent 'make-out' parties. A couple of beanbag chairs quickly turned this store-room-cum-freezer-store into a den of iniquity. 'The girls usually overdid it with that flavoured lip gloss,' recalled Pitt. 'But we didn't know it at the time, we thought it was fine!'

But Jane Pitt didn't think it was at all fine and felt the need to keep an eye on the young man surrounded by the adoring school girls in the basement. 'My mom always made a lot of noise before opening the door to the basement. She'd call down, "Brad? Can I come down and get something out of the freezer?" Of course, you had to wonder why mom needed a frozen steak at 10 o'clock at night...'

Pam Senter, who didn't herself have a romance with Pitt, recalled the girls he was involved with. 'There were plenty of them - girls fell all over him,' she remembers. 'He had real charm and a way with women. I made sure not to fall in love with Brad - I knew he'd break my heart. That's just the way he is, he can't help himself. Yet his parents kept him on a short leash. He didn't run wild and he certainly wasn't promiscuous or anything like that.'

Other youthful, short-lived mid-teen relationships followed Kim Bell and Sara Hart. Following Tonya Westphalen, a neighbour in Springfield, was Lisa Stanzer, a girl who caused something of a falling-out between Brad and younger brother Doug. Brad was first to go out with her, but she soon decided she preferred Doug. Brad still sees a lot of her – she married Doug and they now have a young family of their own in Springfield.

All in all, Brad Pitt enjoyed a normal, happy, contented American childhood and adolescence, growing up in a secure and loving environment in the 1970s. What could possibly make this young man suddenly give everything up and flee to Hollywood in search of those most elusive of goals – fame and fortune?

The fact that William Bradley Pitt would go to college was never up for discussion as he was always scoring good grades. It was the expected thing, and thus far in his short life Brad had always done the expected thing without fail. His

Early publicity shot taken in 1988 in Los Angeles.

late teenage years into his early 20s would be no different, believed his loving parents. However, as he got older, Pitt had begun to question his circumstances. He looked twice at his parents' religion, their beliefs and practices. He looked twice at Springfield, Missouri and what it had to offer him. He looked twice at his parents' jobs, their lives, their dedication to their children, and he began to have second thoughts. Perhaps – just perhaps – the expected middle-class American path through life was not for him, after all? He began to develop a feeling for the wider world beyond Springfield. He wanted to get out there and explore it.

Off he went, as the dutiful son, in 1982 to the University of Missouri at Columbia, over 150 miles from home, to study journalism. At least he was getting a taste of the wider world, while still fulfilling his parents' expectations. Having passed his driving test, that adolescent rite of passage in America, Pitt had inherited an old beat up Buick Centurion 455 from his father, giving him independent mobility.

Independence was very much on his mind - although upon arrival at college he quickly began to fit in with the Animal House stereotypes by moving into a frat house and joining the Sigma Chi fraternity. Escaping the supervision of his parents meant a few wild weeks for Pitt, until the pressures of his student work made him quickly pay more attention to his studies. His interest and stated career aim was in doing 'something in advertising,' which was covered by his course, rather than straightforward mainstream journalism. That seriousness didn't stop him, however, becoming something of a well-known figure on campus when he posed, shirt off, for a student calendar. The news of his baby-faced good looks and muscular physique had already spread around the university and Pitt now enjoyed something of a first taste – albeit in a minor way – of the fame that he was to enjoy world wide in years to come. As with his Best Dressed Student award and The Brief Boys antics at school, he was using his physique in a calculated way to his own advantage.

His friend from school Greg Pontious recalled Pitt in action: 'In our first year of college we put on a charity strip show,' he claimed. 'Hundreds of girls paid to watch Brad – he was the hottest guy in the county. We didn't strip completely naked, but the girl's got their money's worth...' Brad Pitt had just enjoyed his first taste of the adulation that could come from performing.

The escape from his parents also allowed Pitt to scrutinise his religious beliefs more closely, away from the hothouse Baptist atmosphere of his home in Springfield. Free to consider what he'd been taught growing up – and to look at alternatives – Pitt decided he'd lost what little faith he may have had. In fact, he doubted he'd ever truly believed anything for himself, he'd instead been following his parents' lead – after all, he was young and didn't know any better. At college, he was surrounded by so many diverse influences and thoughts he could no longer believe in his parents' 'given' faith without question.

'One of the most pivotal moments I've had was when I finally couldn't buy the religion I grew up with,' recalled Pitt of his university-inspired independent thinking. 'That was a big deal – it was a relief in a way. I didn't have to believe that any more, but then I felt alone. It was this thing I was dependent on.'

Examing his religion put Pitt ahead of his parents for once – a few years later Bill and Jane reconsidered their own commitment and left the Baptist faith to join a non-denominational church.

These years at university saw Pitt develop the laid back attitude, his almost Zen-

Even in his first years in Los Angeles Brad could win comparisons with James Dean.

like view of life, that was to stand him in good stead in Hollywood. This developing 'go with the flow' mentality would allow the actor to take chances at the beginning of his career and to not stick too closely to what he knew was a tried and tested formula. His relaxed approach was to be the key secret to his success in Hollywood and to the attraction that emanated from the cinema screen whenever he appeared.

One particular incident during his university period made Brad Pitt aware of his own mortality. Touring the Columbia countryside with a gang of frat friends, he wrote off the Buick he'd inherited from his father in a collision with a huge out-of-control truck. All in the car escaped from the crash with their lives, even though the collision sheared the roof off the strongly built vehicle.

The crash focused Pitt's thoughts on his future, on whether he was really happy in the path he was following in life. Was he going down this road because he wanted to, or was he doing it to please his parents, because it was the expected thing? Pitt couldn't help but recall the words of his father Bill when he'd thrown that temper tantrum while playing tennis: 'If you're not having fun, don't do it.'

The shock of the accident didn't stop him from quickly buying a new car, however, a Nissan he dubbed 'Runaround Sue' after the 60s Dion song. He threw himself back into his studies, working harder than ever before and partying harder than ever before. It didn't work, though – he still had that vague dissatisfaction niggling away at the back of his mind, his disenchantment with a future path that seemed clearly marked out for him growing by the month.

Pitt found his attempts to be creative in his advertising studies were being discouraged by his conservative tutors. 'There were doggin' all my ideas. They wanted the straight thing and it was really boring. You keep finding things in little increments,' said Pitt. 'Each one of those little increments led me to saying, You know what? I don't want to do this. I want to go over there and see what that's all about. I was a paper short of finishing. That's kind of a metaphorical gesture.'

Two weeks before graduation in 1986 and actually two papers short of getting his degree in journalism studies, Pitt loaded up Runaround Sue and disappeared from the University of Missouri heading to an uncertain future. 'It was such a relief. I was coming to the end of college and the end of my degree and the beginning of my chosen occupation.'

Pitt seemed to feel he'd got all he wanted or needed from his college years, with or without the bit of paper at the end of it that said he was qualified. With his interest in a conventional career and a conventional life waning, these life lessons seemed more important than his qualifications. 'I had a great time in college. I learned more about being on my own than anything from a book. It's just as important to find out what you don't want to do as what you do want to do. I decided everyone was either getting married or applying for jobs, and I didn't want to do either.'

The car crash had served to concentrate his mind and made him pay more attention to the voice in his head telling him there was more to life and he had to go out and get it. The crisis of confidence and faith that Brad Pitt faced as he neared the end of his college education was not all that unusual – but his response to that crisis was. His answer to the eternal question of 'What do I want to do with my life' was to pick up sticks and drive from Missouri to Los Angeles with the intention of becoming an actor in Hollywood.

Why acting and why movies? What made this admittedly charming, but not very experienced 22 year old suddenly want to go to Hollywood, to follow in the well-worn footsteps of many would-be stars, most of whom had failed?

Pitt seems to have been inspired by his teenage trips to local Springfield movie houses with girlfriend Sara Hart and his family. The films he saw stuck in his mind, and he'd realised that acting was one way he could use his personality and his good looks to earn a living. Winning recognition from his peers at school and college by being named Best Dressed Student, selected for the calendar and entertaining with a strip show, reinforced his awareness of his physical self. All those factors were combined with a mounting dissatisfaction with the mundane life that seemed to have been mapped out for him, an increasing curiosity about the world away from his family and friends and an almost naive, but refreshing, belief in himself and his unproven abilities. Taken together it all seems to have been more than enough, in May 1986, to propel Brad Pitt westward to the star-lined streets of Hollywood to try his luck.

2 On TV in LA

FROM across the United States, and indeed from across the world, people have relocated to Hollywood for almost a century hoping that they will be the one from all the wannabes that finally makes the big time. For most of them the reality is to join all the waiters, drivers and low-paid service industry workers who harbour unfulfilled ambitions to be a screenwriter, an actor or a director. Initially, for Brad Pitt this hard reality was to be no different.

University had given Pitt a feel for the wider world. He knew there was something more out there than either Springfield or Columbia could offer him. But he also knew that throwing away his religion and his education to pursue some pipe dream of Hollywood stardom would not go down well with his parents, so he decided to not let on to them what his true aim in California was. As far as Bill and Jane Pitt knew, their son was off to Pasadena to continue his studies at the Art Centre College of Design, a perfectly plausible move to follow up his supposed career direction towards the art side of the advertising industry.

Despite his anticipation of the good life ahead, Los Angeles didn't make that great an impression on its newest arrival in 1986. 'I remember being so excited as I passed each state line,' recalled Pitt in *Rolling Stone*. Accompanied on the long trip only by his Led Zeppelin, Jimi Hendrix, Lynryd Skynyrd and Three Dog Night tapes, he stopped off to see some sights on the way, including the Grand Canyon and some spectacular meteor craters. But then: 'I drove in through Burbank, and the smog was so thick that it seemed like fog. I pulled in and went to McDonalds, and that was it. I just thought, "Shouldn't there be a little more?"'

If the city made a disappointing first impression on the 22-year-old, the job options that seemed available to him were even more disappointing. With only $325 in his pockets, Pitt was faced with finding work rapidly in order to afford the basics of life. He quickly joined the ranks of the Hollywood wannabes toiling in the service industry, hoping against hope for that ever-elusive big break.

Pitt started in a world he knew, delivering refrigerators to college students, just like those he'd left behind. It was hard, physical work, but he didn't mind, and it helped keep him in shape. Next on the thankless task list was a stint at telemarketing – sitting on the telephone all day, calling people to sell them things they didn't want and didn't need. It wasn't the back-breaking work of the delivery business, but it was equally frustrating. At least he was paying the rent and finding his feet in Los Angeles.

He soon found himself socialising and enjoying the opportunities Los Angeles had to offer in his spare time. He was not slow in making new friends, and in frequenting gigs and venues where bands played, he was quickly hanging out with a crowd of musicians. However, although he played guitar and dabbled with the idea of actually getting a band together, recalling his teen rock'n'roll ambitions, Pitt didn't want anything to distract him from his main aim of becoming an actor.

Brad Pitt's first performing role in Los Angeles was as a giant chicken, promoting the Mexican fast food chain El Pollo Loco. It may have been demeaning and far from the kind of performance parts he was hoping to secure, but it was a start of a sort. He'd never performed professionally, never played in theatre beyond the annual efforts at school. He had to get used to doing daft things if he was really going to make it. So, every day he dolled himself up in the yellow feathered costume and became a dancing chicken, welcoming customers into the restaurant at the intersection of Sunset Strip and La Brea Boulevard.

'It was nine dollars an hour,' recalled Pitt. 'That's a lot of money when you're used to making $3.50 for bus boy jobs.' He managed to put up with the insults and jibes that some of the more rowdy customers threw his way, because he felt protected inside the costume. 'I didn't care. They weren't yelling at me, they were yelling at the damn chicken.'

Another of these undemanding jobs was to give him the lead he needed into the real Hollywood world. In the evenings he was putting his driving skills to good use for a strip-o-gram firm. 'That was a good job,' he later remembered in Britain's *Empire* Magazine. 'There were some interesting rides home... I'd drive them there in my car. We'd have a private room. They'd come out and I'd introduce them and play the music – most of them wanted Prince, whatever the "fuck me" songs were – and they'd take their clothes off and throw them my way so guys wouldn't steal them.' It was the first, but not the last, time that strange women would be throwing their clothes at Brad Pitt. At least it beat being a performing chicken.

One of his stripper passengers was to give him his first useful pointer in the right direction. She referred him to a Los Angeles acting coach named Roy London. London was the man who'd given actresses such as Michelle Pfeiffer and Sharon Stone their early career guidance.

Roy London quickly recognised his newest pupil's strong points. He had the good looks that Hollywood liked, certainly at this stage teen idol if not leading man potential, but much more than mere good looks would be required. London took him in hand and guided him in technique. He taught him the basics of the dramatic method and guided him through the duplicitous world of Hollywood agents and casting executives. The young would-be-actor was quick to learn, and he discovered as much about the business side of acting as about dramatic techniques. Soon, Pitt was starting to attend auditions, thanks to London's advice and guidance.

His first exposure to this world was to accompany one of London's other pupils, a young actress, to an audition so he could help her out by reading the male role. The audition was not for a part but to be taken on by a Hollywood agent, the kind of person every young actor needs to fight their corner for them and win them parts. Pitt was relaxed about the whole thing – after all, he wasn't auditioning, he was just helping out a friend. As a result, he was the one the agent wanted to sign, not the actress. His natural abilities shone through because he wasn't really trying. He had set himself a limit of a year in Hollywood. If by then he was not making progress he'd give it all up and head back to the safe, normal life that he knew awaited him back in Springfield, Missouri. That was to be his insurance policy. Now, with an agent behind him, he might not need to call on it.

Pitt started going to auditions more frequently, working them around his continuing bread-and-butter costume chicken and driving duties. Then he started getting second call backs and was beginning to be seriously considered for parts in movies and TV series. His first part was working as a mere extra, but it was a start.

It seems incredible that Brad's first paid acting role was in a huge chicken costume publicising a restaurant.

He appeared in a crowd scene as a preppie standing in a doorway complete with a ponytail and charcoal grey suit in the 1987 movie version of Bret Easton Ellis' nihilistic novel *Less Than Zero*. The film featured several Brat Pack names – young, up-and-coming actors like Andrew McCarthy, Robert Downey Jnr and James Spader. Pitt desperately wanted to count himself as one of them, but a few hours work with the rest of the 'backgrounders' just didn't cut it. For Pitt, though, it was a beginning.

Other bit parts started coming, including a part as a waiter 'in this bad Charlie Sheen movie'. The film was *No Man's Land*, about Los Angeles car thieves; it didn't exactly set the box office alight, but at least Pitt was putting himself about a bit.

After six months in Los Angeles Pitt was making progress. All he needed now was a decent role, something that would get him noticed. His agent and Roy London had suggested TV series as places to develop a good grounding in basic dramatic skills. Guest shots or even a regular part on a series or soap would allow the young actor to try out the business, to see whether he really was cut out for the back-biting world of Hollywood. At six foot tall and with long blond hair and square-jawed face and muscular build, he knew he had the looks to succeed, enough people had told him that, but what Brad Pitt was unsure about was whether he would also have the necessary talent to bring his characters to life.

His first big break came on a handful of episodes of *Dallas*, the high-rating fantasy soap opera that had become a staple of American television in the 80s. Pitt auditioned for a part that was intended to be a short-lived character. He was called back a second time and finally won the role. 'I was in three episodes, probably for about a total of four minutes. I was some reject boyfriend, an idiot. I just had to sit there on the couch and smile and shit,' said Pitt disparagingly of his first TV role.

His character was the brainless but extremely good-looking boyfriend of the daughter of the character played by Priscilla Presley. The daughter's part was

A small part in *Dallas* gave Brad his first widespread exposure and his first serious girlfriend, Shalane McCall.

Brad started getting bit parts within a few months of moving to Hollywood.

played by Shalane McCall, and the fake on-screen romance soon spilled over into a real-life off-screen entanglement. At 23, Pitt enjoyed his first adult affair. However, he wasn't the clichéd predatory actor, bedding his co-stars just for the sake of it. In fact, he appears to have been seduced by McCall, but the relationship only lasted six weeks. Once Pitt finished his part on the show and began again to separate reality from the TV fantasy, he called it off. According to *The National Enquirer*, McCall was devastated by the break-up, having taken the relationship much more seriously than Pitt appeared to have done.

Phil Lobel, Pitt's personal manager from 1987, when he did *Dallas*, through to about 1989, felt the young actor was particularly vulnerable compared with those who had survived the Hollywood feeding frenzy for a few years. 'He fell in love very easily,' said Lobel of his charge. According to the agent, Pitt had a habit of buying his girlfriends numerous, expensive gifts which ate into his meagre acting earnings, and he would finance some of these early infatuations by offering the actor loans to be paid back out of his earnings.

'I've never seen Brad try and get a girl to go home with him,' recalled an anonymous friend in a *People* magazine profile. 'They come to him. He's actually kinda shy.' Like most things in his 23 years so far, romance and women also seemed to come too easily to Brad Pitt. Among those who fell into his bed during his early struggling years in Los Angeles was British pop star Sinitta. 'We only had a brief affair,' she later admitted, 'but it was wonderfully passionate...'

Finally, Pitt was winning enough bit parts to give up the chicken and stripper chauffeuring businesses altogether. He could now pay his rent from his acting income. He had proved to himself he could do it. It was time to call his parents and tell them what he was really up to. 'Yeah, I thought so,' was Bill Pitt's fatherly comment when Brad finally came clean about his acting life. He had been fooling no-one.

He also told some of his old friends at the University of Missouri in Columbia what he was really doing in Los Angeles. 'People at Missouri were really surprised when they found out what Brad was doing,' claimed Pitt's University friend Chris Schudy in *Rolling Stone*. 'But he's always been so charming that it made some sense. The first time my mom met him, she called him a little Roman god.'

Pitt's later fame was to have quite an effect on the population of his old Alma Mater. Four of Pitt's Sigma Chi buddies have followed in his footsteps to Hollywood - although none have hustled as far and a fast as Pitt managed.

Following *Dallas*, Pitt won a week of work in a daytime soap *Another World*, a well-worn proving ground for many young actors and actresses who went on to better things on TV and in movies. He was happy to pay his dues in these parts - they kept him working, earning income and they kept his face and his resumé in front of the town's casting directors.

More short-lived roles followed, including a stint on the sitcom *Growing Pains*, which was later to launch the career of Leonardo DiCaprio. In an episode entitled 'Who's Zoomin' Who?' with Lisa Capp and Kevin Wixted, Pitt played Jeff, a new student at the school where the teen sitcom was set. Playing up his affinity with James Dean, Jeff does his best to seduce Carol (Tracey Gold) away from her boyfriend Bobby (Wixted). The episode included Pitt taking Gold to a screening of Dean's *Rebel Without a Cause* (1955). The episode, originally transmitted on 10th November 1987, featured Pitt in what would quickly become his standard hunky

Brad was determined to break into movies right from the time he left Missouri.

high-schooler TV mode.

The action-adventure series *21 Jump Street* - the series that turned actor Johnny Depp into an international heart throb - also featured a guest appearance from Pitt. In 1988, *21 Jump Street* producer Patrick Hapsburgh prefigured the later thoughts of *thirtysomething*'s Edward Zwick when he recognised Pitt's presence on the show. 'Brad walking into a room was more exciting than most actors doing a scene.'

In episode 33 of *21 Jump Street*, entitled 'Best Years of Your Life' premiered on 1st May 1988, Pitt appeared alongside Cheryl Pollak in a story that explored how the suicide of a popular student - whom Hanson (Johnny Depp) and Penhall (Peter DeLuise) had arrested the night before - leaves his family, fellow students and Hanson in a state of depression and forces Penhall to relive bitter childhood memories of his own mother's suicide. Pitt got to play some lunch room scenes opposite Depp.

A brief part on the TV drama *thirtysomething* followed. 'I had no lines,' remembered Pitt. 'Actually, I think I had one line. It was 'No' or 'Yes'. I can't remember. These are not monumental moments we're talking about here.' His moment on the *thirtysomething* episode entitled 'Love and Sex' (broadcast on 3rd October 1989) may not have been monumental to Pitt, but his presence did impress the TV series creators Edward Zwick and Marshall Herskovitz, who said 'He caused such a stir on the set. He was so good looking and charismatic and such a sweet guy, everybody knew he was going places.' Playing the boyfriend of Cheryl Pollak's baby-sitter character, Pitt got to ride around on a motorbike and wear black leathers. He had a presence in the episode, but the character had next to no dialogue, requiring very little acting from Pitt and a lot more posing. The part, though, made connections forwards and backwards with Pitts career: Zwick was to cast him in the epic *Legends of the Fall* several years later, and Cheryl Pollak, who played the baby-sitter, had also been Pitt's girlfriend in the episode of *21 Jump Street* he had been in.

Although all these jobs were minor efforts, Pitt was very pleased to be doing them, even if he played high school kids in almost all of them. 'I was thinking "This is great!" I come from the Ozark Mountains. We don't have that kind of stuff where I grew up. I move out there [Hollywood] and all of a sudden I'm in the middle of it. Fantastic!' However, while happy to be having some success, Pitt was not so laid back that he was going to put all his career eggs into the Hollywood basket. He may have been hasty enough to leave his university two weeks away from graduation, but he did regard continuing his education as important, just in case the acting thing didn't work out. To that end, Pitt continued during his early days in Hollywood to teach himself about art, architecture and design. At auditions he would often be seen sitting waiting for his call, sketch book and pencil in hand, using his waiting time to productive ends.

Phil Lobel suggested more sitcoms like *Growing Pains* rather than soaps like *Another World*, so Pitt found himself playing for a few weeks in episodes of *Head of the Class*, a high school comedy show. It wasn't the kind of role that he wanted to play any longer, but his romantic instincts led him to an affair with the co-star on *Head of the Class*, Robin Givens. They began a passionate, if short-lived, relationship. Pitt knew who Givens was from the news coverage of her split from boxer husband Mike Tyson, and at the time that Pitt joined the cast of *Head of the*

Class Givens was on the rebound. The pair dated for six months, and Pitt found himself on the roster of subjects making the gossip columns of not only the Hollywood trade press and local Los Angeles newspapers, but national entertainment magazines like *People* and *Entertainment Weekly*. The experience revealed to Pitt that you didn't even have to be a star to make the papers – simply date one and you're there.

According to *People* magazine, Pitt even encountered Mike Tyson during a romantic visit to Robin Givens' home. As the magazine put it 'Givens's fast talking preserved Pitt's profile'. His liaison with Givens gave Pitt a boost up the career ladder – and he hadn't even played a high-profile part either on TV or in a movie yet. He now had a public presence in the entertainment press.

Success seemed to be falling into Pitt's lap. His progress up the Hollywood chain was seemingly effortless. He had swiftly moved from being an unknown with no track record and no experience to being a recognised TV face with a significant handful of sit-coms and soap opera credits to his name. His agents, advisors and Pitt himself clearly saw the next step. He had to make the move away from TV into films, to build on and extend his limited success so far.

3 Making Movies

A S IT turned out Brad Pitt's first feature-length project was for television, despite his desire to get away from the small screen.

A Stoning in Fulham County was a 1988 TV movie starring TV names Jill Eikenberry and Ken Olin (from *thirtysomething*), but to Brad Pitt it was another opportunity to work – and at least it wasn't another one-off TV series episode.

As it turned out *A Stoning in Fulham County* was an above-average example of the TV movie-of-the-week-genre. Directed by Larry Elikmann from an intelligent and provocative script by Jud Kinberg and Jackson Gillis, the film tells the story of how an Amish family whose baby child is killed in an incident of religious harassment refuses to bring the case to trial. Pitt felt familiar with some of the religious issues from his own family background.

Pitt played Teddy Johnson, one of four Fulham County youths engaged in a long-standing local practice of harassing the Amish population. Their stone-throwing ambush on an Amish family in their horse-and-cart results in the death of the family's seven-month-old daughter. A reluctant participant, Pitt's character shows remorse afterwards in a key scene in which he and his mother visit the Amish family. The main thrust of the plot follows the prosecutor's attempt to persuade the family to give evidence in court and so convict the two boys who threw the stones.

The star of the film was Ron Perlman, more famous as the beastly star of the romantic fantasy TV series *Beauty and the Beast*, as the Amish father. Brad Pitt got to work again alongside actor Nicholas Pryor, as the cocky defence attorney, who had featured in *Less Than Zero*. It was a small part, but the film as a whole was a good piece of work for Pitt to be associated with.

He followed *A Stoning in Fulham County* with his first sizeable part in a real film, although 1989's *Cutting Class* was more than likely destined for video hell and drive-in theatres than respectable movie houses.

A cheap and not-so-cheerful horror spoof, *Cutting Class* set out to lampoon the likes of the unfathomably popular slasher movies *Friday the 13th* and John Carpenter's *Hallowe'en*. Horror films in general - whether played for laughs or relatively straight - have proved to be a training ground in movies, not only for up-and-coming actors like Brad Pitt, but also for writers and directors who later then go on to much more significant films, either within or outside the genre that spawned them.

Pitt was happy at the time to get third billing in the credits. Later in his career he preferred to forget the movie altogether and leave it off his official resumé, but these things have a habit of catching up with most Hollywood stars. And while not a brilliant piece of entertainment, there is nothing in *Cutting Class* that should unduly embarrass him.

Directed by Rospo Pallenberg, the film is set in a typical American high school, packed to the rafters with the usual round-up of teenage stereotypes - all just waiting to be bumped off. Pitt plays much younger than his 26 years - something he always found easy to do with his baby-face looks. He stars as Dwight, the all-

American good looking basketball team star with everything going for him. He gets to zoom about town in a fashionable red convertible and is dating the school's prettiest cheerleader - played by actress Jill Schoelen, who had played a more significant horror heroine opposite Terry O'Quinn in *The Stepfather* (1987).

Pitt was simply perfect for the part - and it didn't require much effort for him to fulfil the requirements of the role. He was essentially the hero and the comic relief in the plot rolled into one. Someone in the school is murdering the pupils, and the principal suspect is teen psycho Donovan Leitch. As teachers start to get bumped off the film follows Dwight: fumbling the ball at a crucial moment in a big basketball game, getting drunk with his mates (no doubt drawing on his university experiences for that one) and finally becoming the big hero in the end. Also featured in the movie was veteran actor Roddy McDowall, who'd featured in Pitt's favourite film *Planet of the Apes*, and the chance to work with him might have helped Pitt take the decision to do the movie.

Fangoria magazine described the film in its 'Skeletons in the Closet' section which digs out the early horror movie appearances of today's big Hollywood stars. In a review of Pitt's performance writer Steve Puchalski pulled no punches: 'Pitt's early acting ability consisted of a perpetual doe-eyed stare, perfect for this generic role. Present day fans will see a glimmer of the bigger and better things lurking under the surface. But in truth, the most fun will be had by Pitt detractors who'll get a good laugh from seeing his head stuffed painfully into a shop class vise during the climax. Now that's acting!'

Cutting Class introduced another new woman into Brad Pitt's life, co-star Jill Schoelen. Playing Pitt's girlfriend in the film spilled over into real life, as with Shalane McCall on *Dallas* and Robin Givens in *Head of the Class*. And as with the others, this Pitt romance was short-lived – about three months. The pair split up as they built their separate careers.

Brad Pitt's next effort, 1989's *Happy Together*, was not a great deal better than *Cutting Class*. In his *Annual Movie and Video Guide* Leonard Maltin called the film a 'slight, predictable romantic comedy in which college students Patrick Dempsey and Helen Slater are accidentally paired up as roommates. You can just guess how this one turns out.' Helen Slater had played *Supergirl* in the 1984 film, but there's no suggestion that Brad Pitt found the attractive actress as super as some of the others he'd co-starred with.

Patrick Dempsey played Chris, a would-be writer newly arrived at college in Los Angeles, to discover that his room-mate Alex (Helen Slater) is a girl, the housing department having assumed the name to be male. They make the most of the love-hate situation with all the expected dramatic entanglements. The pair share the same drama class, which also features Brad Pitt as another student named Brian. He starts out as Alex's boyfriend until Chris arrives on the scene. The class exercises tried out in these scenes were probably familiar to Pitt from his days with Roy London. There's even a musical interlude where Dempsey and Slater sing 'Life is a Cabaret', but Pitt doesn't get to take part.

His part in *Happy Together* was far smaller than that he'd had in *Cutting Class*, but Pitt was happy to keep working, to keep his face on the screen, whether it was on TV, videos or in cinemas. He and his manager Phil Lobel knew that was the best way for the new boy in town to get noticed. He would only progress up to

Brad Pitt's 'performance' in a Levi's ad as a young jail-breaker armed with a camera and a pair of jeans brought him to the notice of millions across Europe.

bigger and better parts, get auditions for decent films and get more frequent audition call-backs if he became a familiar face within the industry. Brad Pitt was in too much of a hurry to sit back and wait for casting directors to come to him.

Pitt's biggest role to date came in a 1989 episode of the comic-book inspired Home Box Office (HBO) TV series *Tales From the Crypt*. The series was put together by no less than five high-powered film producers – Richard Donner, Walter Hill, David Giler, Joel Silver and Robert Zemeckis – and drew on the best gruesome blackly comic tales from the 50s DC comic book of the same title. The original idea was that as the series was for a cable station the more liberal rules on sex and violence would allow the producers to do justice to the gruesome tales. The results were rather different, unfortunately.

Each half-hour tale of the macabre was introduced by the cadaverous Crypt Keeper, an animatronic puppet. The script packed each introduction and closing scene with cringe-making, horror-inspired gags, before devoting the remaining 25 minutes or so to pedestrian adaptations of the stories with low production values. Later in 1995 the series was to inspire a duo of spin-off movies, starting with the Billy Zane starrer *Demon Knight* and *Bordello of Blood*.

In the episode entitled 'King of the Road', first broadcast on 18th January 1992, Pitt won his first lead role and his first top billing. He played Billy Drake, a stranger newly arrived in Denver. His tattooed, leather-jacket-wearing drop-out drag racer takes an interest in one of the town's most respectable police officers, Garrett. Drake discovers that Garrett has a secret in his past, namely that he was once a famous drag racer called the 'Iceman', and forces him into a final drag race by kidnapping his daughter.

A very thinly disguised homage to *Rebel Without a Cause*, the *Tales From the Crypt* episode brought Brad Pitt the first of many comparisons with James Dean, making him one of many up-and-coming young actors since the mid-80s, from River Phoenix to Johnny Depp, to have been hailed as the 'new James Dean'.

Happy to be playing a leading role, even if it was only in a 30-minute TV episode, Pitt played up the James Dean connection in his performance, giving just a hint of some of the mean and moody elements he would bring to his characters in feature films like *Kalifornia* and *Legends of the Fall* much later in his career.

Pitt's first flash of fame in Europe was to come not from any of his films or TV show appearances, but from an advert for Levi jeans. His all-American looks resulted in Pitt being chosen for a European advertising campaign. The 30-second spot was an instant hit, with Pitt's smouldering appearance not so much selling jeans as selling himself. He played a jail bird breaking out by removing his 501s and tying them to the broken bars of his cell window, to the tune of Marc Bolan's '20th Century Boy'.

It wasn't the first and it wouldn't be the last time that Brad Pitt's looks alone were enough to turn a woman's head - even the most unlikely of candidates. Later with fame came celebrity friends for Pitt, among them gay singer Melissa Etheridge. 'Brad's effect is far reaching. One night a few of us, shall we say, lesbians were in the hot tub watching the guys play basketball in the pool. We were staring at Brad, and we all agreed he could change a woman's mind,' Etheridge was to tell *Vanity Fair* in 1995.

But Pitt was worried about just relying on his looks, and as a result wavered about doing the Levis advert. This early in what was an acting career that was

The other message that was put across was 'Here's a face to remember.'

growing, albeit slowly, did he really want to be known not for his dramatic work, but for taking his clothes off in a jeans advert? 'It's all just a game, isn't,' he mused on the media's concentration on people's surface attributes. 'It's up to you, if you've got anything more in you, it's up to you to show it.' So he took the part – it was a short work schedule for a good return, and rather than damaging his rising reputation, it might actually do him some good. After all, the campaign was only to run on TV screens across Europe. What harm could it do?

None, as it happened. He found himself to be an instant sex symbol across Europe, where none of his movies or TV appearances had yet been seen. It was the best possible outcome - Pitt could continue to pursue meaty dramatic parts in Hollywood, hoping that when the films reached cinemas in Europe he could cash in on being 'the Levi jeans boy'.

Pitt had achieved his aim, making the cross-over from episodic TV work to feature-length films. Although neither *A Stoning in Fulham County* or *Cutting Class* were star-making projects, they did show that he was capable of handling prominent feature-film roles. While he continued to tackle further TV work in the likes of *Tales From the Crypt* and the Levi jeans advert, he could now direct his ambitions to bigger parts in bigger movies.

Pitt also had a more personal concern on his mind. Since his series of affairs with co-stars such as Shalane McCall, Robin Givens, and Jill Schoelen, Pitt had enjoyed no really serious romantic liaisons. He was on the look-out for a partner to share in his adventures in movie making.

4 Juliette

BEFORE PITT could make the final break with TV he was made an offer the young actor found hard to refuse – his own TV series. That a network thought him worthy of having a TV series built around him was a sign to him and his agents that he'd become a name to be reckoned with. His continued willingness to 'pay his dues' in TV was also to lead Pitt into an unexpected long-term romance.

The Fox TV Network was a long-in-the-planning ambition come true for international multi-media baron Rupert Murdoch. Having started by inheriting his father's newspaper business in Australia, Murdoch had expanded his media interests around the globe. From owning newspapers and satellite TV interests in Britain, to papers and local TV stations in America, to a mid-90s expansion in Asian through the Star TV satellite, Murdoch's ambition knew no bounds. In that context, his plan to build a fourth TV network in America to compete with CBS, NBC and ABC was not at all far fetched. After all, Ted Turner had turned a handful of Atlanta local TV stations into Cable News Network (CNN), a well-respected international 24 hour news broadcaster. With his purchase of the 20th Century Fox film studio and a group of local TV stations, Murdoch had the beginnings of what was to become the Fox Network. The only set back was that because of Federal Communications Commission (FCC) cross-media ownership rules he was forced to divest himself of some of his American newspaper interests, as he was forbidden from owning a TV station and newspaper in the same area. This was not a problem a change of citizenship couldn't solve, however.

By the time Brad Pitt was auditioning for the regular lead role on *Glory Days*, a combination of dramatic series and sitcom, the Fox Network had just completed its first year on air. Although the newest American TV channel could lay claim to some instant hits – notably the animated show *The Simpsons*, the comedy *Married...With Children* and the twentysomething soap *Beverly Hills 90210* – it was four years away from its big breakthrough with the likes of the international mega-hit *The X-Files*.

In an attempt to beat the competing networks and make a bit of a PR splash Fox decided to bring its new season programming for 1990 forward from the traditional September start to midsummer, when most stations broadcast wall-to-wall re-runs. Central to this unique – and ultimately doomed strategy was their new comedy-drama *Glory Days*.

The series was an ensemble piece, following the lives of four friends after they'd left high school. Again, Pitt ended up playing significantly younger than his 26 years, but he could still get away with it. There were echoes from his own life in the character he played, Walker Lovejoy, which cemented his commitment to the part and the series. In the show Walker had quit college in a temper tantrum after having problems with the football team. He was now making his way in the world as a junior reporter for a local newspaper. It was a particularly easy part for Pitt to play, as he could draw on both his college experience and the specifics of his journalism studies.

'He was like, organised to a certain extent, and that was really appealing to me.' (Juliette Lewis)

35

Unfortunately such attention to detail would not be required – *Glory Days* was destined for a less than glorious fate, dying an ignominious death after just six episodes. It is the way of American TV to drop shows quickly if they fail to gather a large audience in a short period of time. Fox was feeling the pressure from advertisers, to whom they would have to refund payments if shows failed to reach a certain level of ratings. With a six-episode commitment to the series, the new station promoted the show heavily, but to no avail. Not sure whether it was a comedy or a drama, *Glory Days* was a casualty of a brutal ratings war that meant that even good shows were not given time to find their feet and secure an audience. The series was, in fact, quite good, something of a precursor for later ensemble youth series, though less of a fantasy, but Fox was quick to drop shows prematurely. They were to learn their lessons, however, allowing *The X Files* in 1993 to weather a low-rated first season and to find its audience through word of mouth. But a more brutal attitude still prevailed for *Glory Days* and Brad Pitt's hopes of TV stardom.

Pitt was upset about the series being cancelled. He saw the show as a chance to reinforce his acting credentials. He had hoped to stay on it for at least one season, then segue into movies on the back of a successful TV series, just as he'd seen other actors do – notably Johnny Depp, from *21 Jump Street*. But it wasn't to be, and Pitt faced a few more years toiling in the world of B-movies and TV movie-of-the-week productions, although to his relief, the quality of the scripts he was being offered started to improve after *Glory Days*.

The chance to work alongside British actor Albert Finney attracted Brad Pitt to a small role in the Home Box Office 1990 TV movie *The Image*.

The drama was a lighter version of Paddy Chayefsky's 1970s film *Network*, about the power of television and those who report the news. Albert Finney played Jason Cromwell, the self-obsessed and driven anchor of a TV show *Here and Now*. Drifting apart from his theatre director wife Jean (Marsha Mason) and into the arms of his researcher Marcie Guildford (Kathy Baker, from TV's *Picket Fences*), Cromwell is under great pressure – he is held to be the most trusted man on American television. Cromwell has a closer relationship with his producer Irv Mickleson (John Mahoney, who now plays Kelsey Grammer's father on the TV sitcom *Frasier*) than with his wife, even though Irv has a tendency to chat to a giant stuffed bear.

Among the stories investigated by the *Here and Now* team are a 'Dr Death' character, a Texan Savings and Loan scandal and a bunch of neo-Nazi skinheads. Things go wrong on the Savings and Loan story, though, when an innocent man accused by *Here and Now* of defrauding the bank commits suicide. After the death of Irv Mickleson in a plane crash, and with station boss Frank Goodrich (a cameo by Spalding Gray) trying to get Cromwell off current affairs and into lifestyle journalism and celebrity interviews, Cromwell sets out to re-investigate the story and right a few wrongs.

On his own in Texas, Cromwell hires the services of a local cowpoke cameraman named Steve Black. Enter Brad Pitt, billed 15th in the credits and on screen for less than ten minutes. However, all his scenes, from their meeting in a car park, to his filming Cromwell's interviews and supplying pizzas and VCRs to the TV anchor, are with Finney exclusively. In retrospect, the part looks like a dry run for JD in *Thelma & Lousie*, with Pitt putting on a Texan accent, ten gallon hat, denim

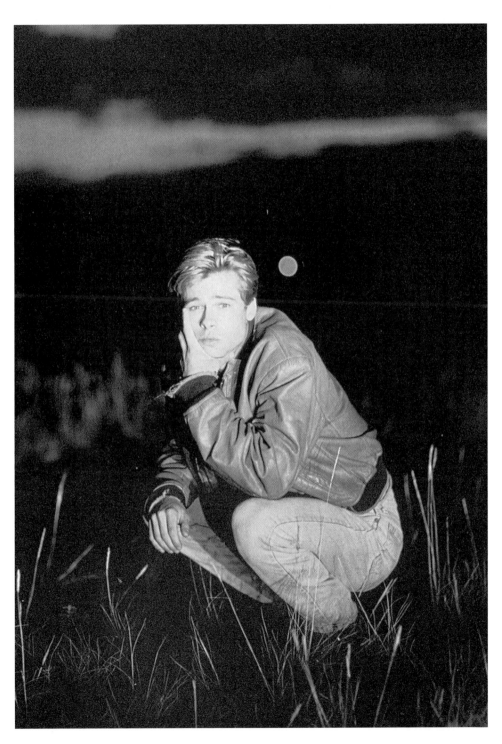

Brad's resemblance in his early twenties to the young Robert Redford was noted by
many, including, to Brad's later benefit, the actor-director himself.

jacket, jeans and pony-tail.

After his two HBO outings in the *Tales From the Crypt* episode and *The Image*, Pitt once again escaped TV movie land in the low-budget cinema feature film *Across the Tracks* in 1990.

The one problem as far as Pitt was concerned was that he was playing younger than his true age yet again. The character of Joe, a high school athlete, was not going to be one that would allow the actor to stretch his abilities. He'd simply be repeating some of the moves he'd made in his previous work. However, this was a real film again, and he wasn't in a position to turn down work, no matter how much he might dislike the part.

The star was Rick Schroder, playing Billy Maloney, and Pitt was cast as Joe Maloney, his younger brother. Their mother was played by Carrie Snodgrass. Billy is the proverbial kid from the wrong side of the tracks, returning home at the beginning of the movie after serving time in jail for auto theft. Pitt's character is the pride and joy of the Maloney family, a good athlete who has kept his nose clean and is bound to make something of his life. With second billing on offer and almost as much screen time as Schroder, Pitt had quickly committed to the project.

In the film, when older brother Billy returns home, he begins to have a distracting effect on younger brother Joe. While Joe concentrates on school and his efforts to win an athletic scholarship to Stanford, Billy is returning to his old criminal ways. When Billy finally cleans up his act and shows Joe he's probably the better athlete, it's enough to make Joe lose heart and almost throw in his struggle to make his life work out.

The part required some physical dedication from Pitt, who was now well out of condition. For all the running and jumping he'd be doing Pitt had to get back into some serious training.

Across the Tracks was shot locally in California, its low budget prohibiting any kind of travel further afield. That suited Pitt as he wanted to stay close to what was now his own turf – he never knew when another audition opportunity might come up.

Shooting in the summer, during school vacation when the production could use a local high school, took its toll on the cast, mainly the major stars who had to perform their athletic feats with the hot sun beating down on them. It was the only minor inconvenience in what was otherwise an easy shoot for Pitt. Joe was so much like his earlier self that the actor was able to draw directly on his own high school and college days – not so much for the emotions of the story which came clearly through from Sandy Tung's script, but for the feel of being a high schooler with ambitions beyond his immediate environment.

Joe Maloney was the biggest role Pitt had enjoyed to date. It meant learning many more lines – although Joe was the first in a long line of Pitt characters who don't say much but communicate better through their eyes than with their words. He was to be on screen throughout much of the film, and, although he had second billing, his character was clearly the main focus of the drama. Although *Across the Tracks* was never destined to be a big hit in the cinema, with no stars to speak of and a less than spectacular story, it was to win a well deserved afterlife on video and TV, where the more intimate nature of the drama worked better. From Pitt's point of view the film was a good calling card to have before the casting directors of

Hollywood. It proved to them that he could hold a performance for the full length of a feature film, after his TV roles and 10 minute stint in *The Image*. It showed he could hold his own up against seasoned performers like Schroder and Snodgrass, and it showed that he was potentially much more than just a pretty face, if he was to be given the right role.

After *Across the Tracks*, Brad Pitt found himself back in TV Movie of the Week territory once again for the issue-based drama *Too Young to Die?*. It was a move backwards, but he was not to regret it, as during the production he was to meet young actress Juliette Lewis.

Juliette Lewis's early life was very different from Pitt's. She was born into a Hollywood family, being the daughter of actor Geoffrey Lewis and Glenis Batley, a graphic artist. Unlike Pitt, who decided to pursue acting almost on the spur of the moment (Pitt called it 'a quick decision that took me 22 years to make'), Lewis had started her acting career at the age of 12, in Showtime's mini-series *Homefires*. However, as Pitt was to do after her, Lewis guest-starred in TV series, and she won a recurring role in *The Wonder Years*.

Again, like Pitt, she starred in a cheesy horror movie spoof early in her career, enjoying fifth billing in 1988 aged 14 in the weird *Meet the Hollowheads*, alongside John Glover and the wonderfully named Bobcat Goldthwait. The same year she won legal emancipation from her parents, not because she wanted to escape the family home but simply so she could be employed to act full time as an adult, giving her exemption from the restrictive child labour laws, and freedom from the requirement of having an on-set tutor.

Bigger and better things awaited her in a star-making turn as the object of Robert DeNiro's desires in the Martin Scorsese thriller *Cape Fear* (1991), leading to parts in Woody Allen's *Husbands and Wives* (1992), *Romeo Is Bleeding* (1994), *Kalifornia* (1994) again opposite Brad Pitt, and in Oliver Stone's controversial *Natural Born Killers* (1994).

Back in 1990, though, Lewis was trapped in TV work alongside Pitt. There were ten years between them - she was 16, Pitt 26, but they were cast as a couple of contemporary characters involved in the drug scene for *Too Young to Die?*.

The movie was drawn from a real-life case that raised the issue of the legal age of responsibility and whether the death sentence could be applied to minors. Lewis played the main part of 14-year-old Amanda Sue Bradley, a teenager living with her mother and stepfather in an Oklahoma trailer park. Abused by her stepfather, she had tried to escape through a short-lived marriage to her high school sweetheart. When it failed, she returned home, only to find her parents gone and herself abandoned.

Hanging around an army base Amanda Sue soon joins up with Billy (Pitt), a local wide boy who gets her hooked on drugs and into his bed. She escapes again, to be taken in by a sympathetic army sergeant who quickly has to give her up when his superiors find out about the underage girl looking after his kids.

After she returns to the abusive Billy, the two of them fall back into drugs and hatch a plot to kidnap Amanda Sue's army sergeant lover. Once they have done that, Billy encourages Amanda Sue to stab him, making her guilty of murder.

This was controversial stuff for a TV movie and Brad Pitt knew when he received the script that he'd be dumb to turn it down. Here was a production that was bound to get a lot of press coverage and be discussed on daytime talk shows. The part of Billy was one that might just bring him the recognition he sought and allow him to branch out from the teens and high schooler parts he'd been stuck with.

The part of Billy in *Too Young to Die?* was a far cry from the sympathetic role he'd played in *Across the Tracks* or any of the other roles he'd previously played on TV and in movies. He was a down-and-out bum living out of a car, involved in drugs and the driving force behind the murder of the army officer, and fundamentally a coward who then tries to blame the whole thing on Amanda Sue. This was not easy stuff for an actor of limited experience who'd previously drawn on his own life to inspire his high school characters. For once, Brad Pitt really had to stretch to find the part within himself.

Although unsympathetic, Billy had to be given some charisma so as to explain why Amanda Sue returned to him and stayed with him. He had to be both disgusting and repulsive as well as attractive to the main character. It was a tall order, but Pitt saw in the role an opportunity finally to exercise his dramatic muscles and prove to himself, if no-one else, that he could handle this kind of complicated role.

After having pumped up for *Across the Tracks*, Pitt quickly set about reversing his athletic physique for the new role. He thinned himself down and grew a straggly, scruffy blond beard. Although he drew his initial inspiration for Billy from the script by David Hill and George Rubino, Pitt brought much more to the role than either the scriptwriters or director Robert Markowitz anticipated. His thinking about the character and his natural abilities brought Billy to life in a way that some other actors might not have. He succeeded in pulling off the tricky combination of characteristics that the part required, but he also displayed something else more unexpected: an emerging star power.

Brad Pitt got more out of *Too Young to Die?* than a mere glimmering of his own developing talents - he also won himself a girlfriend in the shape of Juliette Lewis. 'It wasn't until shooting ended that we realised we wanted to spent more time together,' said Lewis of the way the relationship developed.

During filming Pitt had no real thoughts of having a romance with Lewis – she was ten years younger than him and the theme of the piece was not really conducive to romance. As Pitt said, tongue firmly in cheek, 'It was quite romantic, shooting her full of drugs and stuff.'

However, although neither of them was looking for it, a romance did blossom. The pair did research together and got closer doing the work. 'We got together to look at *Panic in Needle Park* (1971) for research 'cause we had a shooting-up scene,' Lewis told *Rolling Stone* magazine. 'We hung out in this hotel room in Taft, outside of LA, watching this movie. I noticed he had this black luggage, real organised. Matching. I have three different bags from all over. He had a CD case – I hadn't even moved up from tapes yet. He was like, organised to a certain extent, and that was really appealing to me. He was just really authentic.'

Spending two hours driving back to LA from Taft the pair had more time to get to know each other away from the pressures of the movie set. 'We didn't say much,' recounted Lewis. 'We listened to music. After that drive we both knew we liked each other. We didn't even kiss. I was expecting it, because you move so fast these days. But he didn't – he gave me a hug. I tortured my best friend Trish [Merkens, her flatmate] over this for the next three weeks.'

Brad Pitt had to stretch himself to play the part of a druggy down-and-out who nevertheless exercised a charismatic hold on Juliette Lewis's Amanda Sue.

Brad Pitt spent those three weeks thinking about Juliette Lewis, trying to decide how to handle his feelings for her. He was used to having women around him, and had enjoyed several adult relationships since high school but nothing was as intense as his feelings for Lewis. He was worried, though, about their age difference. It wasn't so much the fact that there was ten years between them, but simply the fact that Juliette was so young. At 16 she still had a lot to learn about life and love. However, Pitt convinced himself that she was mature for her age and decided to take the plunge. He'd thought about how a serious romance would affect his plans for a career in Hollywood, but decided that, as they were both pursuing the same goal, it would be good to share his life with someone he had so much in common with professionally, even if they came from very different backgrounds.

After production wrapped on *Too Young to Die?*, Pitt and Lewis moved in to a one-bedroom rented bungalow in Los Angeles. Soon the small property was cluttered with both their belongings. It was the first time either of them had lived with someone else, and it was a struggle at first getting used to having someone around a lot of the time. In among the usual clutter that any young couple would gather were scripts for forthcoming projects to be read and either committed to or rejected, glossy 8 by 10 pictures of each of them, and invitations to auditions. Both had career paths they were trying to carve out, and it was helpful to have the other one around to bounce ideas off and to get a second opinion on potential scripts.

In a 1991 feature on Lewis, *People* magazine broached the subject of marriage and kids to the couple. Admitting they were 'madly in love', Lewis revealed that the pair expected 'to get married in a few years,' but didn't plan children any time soon.

(Below) Brad and Juliette at home in their small Los Angeles home.

(Opposite) *Too Young to Die* gave Brad the chance to show he could play a scruffy, manipulative character, as well as the clean-cut, athletic types his television work had cast him in previously.

Lewis felt she'd struck gold with Pitt. 'He's like a painting,' she told *People*. 'I wasn't looking for that, he just came that way.' Career jealousy was not something that was going to affect them. 'I'd like nothing better than for him to become the next Robert Redford,' she said presciently. 'If he started getting mobbed whenever we go out, sure, that would be annoying. It already is. But he's not turned on by anonymous pretty bodies. They're just bodies...'

As for Brad Pitt's opinion – well, he was going with the flow, off to wherever the moment was to take him. It was a strategy that had served him well so far. Like his decision to give up college and come to LA in search of an acting career, he decided to move in with Juliette Lewis because at that moment it felt like the right thing to do. Living with her became something of an easy-come-easy-go experience. The grungy Hollywood couple that Pitt and Lewis were in the process of becoming in the press was just how they were in real life, not a contrived image manufactured by some PR consultant. 'Maybe it's because we're pigs,' joked Pitt with *The Village Voice*. 'I don't think it's a conscious choice. But I believe in Wallabees [a make of casual shoes] and boxers [shorts], and she's got her own style too. I'm not going to tell her differently.'

Many people in the Hollywood community were surprised by their teaming up, not just because of the age difference, but because they had totally different types of character. Pitt wasn't to be put off by the gossip mongers, though, commenting on the relationship only by saying, 'We surprise me.'

Things had changed for Pitt again. What he'd hoped to be a hit TV series in *Glory Days* had failed to fly, *The Image* had been something of an indulgence, while *Across the Tracks* had more or less disappeared without trace. It was the sentimental movie of the week *Too Young to Die?* that had got both Pitt and Lewis the best notices of their careers to date. Waiting just around the corner, though, was the role in Ridley Scott's *Thelma & Louise* that was once and for all to catapult him into the role of *bona fide* movie star.

Brad and Juliette at the Academy Awards in 1992.

5 The $6,000 Orgasm

IT WAS a casting call like any other that brought Brad Pitt along to audition for Ridley Scott's new movie. In fact, it looked less promising than most because Pitt's chances of winning the role of JD, a hitch-hiker and small time crook looked remote, simply because he wasn't the first choice. The casting director was straight with the young actor – Ridley Scott wanted William Baldwin, one of the Baldwin brothers acting clan, the most successful of whom had been Alec Baldwin. Pitt thought it was worth trying out for the part anyway – and for a good reason. He was going to be auditioning opposite Geena Davis, one of Hollywood's most gorgeous women stars.

'It just sparked,' said Pitt of his audition with Davis, so it was disappointing to know there was no chance of actually winning the role. It was therefore a pleasant shock when he got a call telling him he was going to play JD after all. Baldwin had pulled out of the film at the last moment to take up a bigger role in Ron Howard's all-star fire-fighting drama *Backdraft* (1991) instead.

British ex-pat film director Ridley Scott started his career in TV commercials, before making his feature film debut with the arty drama *The Duellists* (1977), an adaptation of Joseph Conrad's story of an obsessive feud between two officers during the Napoleonic Wars, starring Harvey Keitel and Keith Carradine. Concentrating on the visuals, rather than the story, Scott's work got noticed and next landed him the directing job on what was intended to be no more than a low-budget horror flick.

The story goes that Scott started on this next film and spent the whole of its budget on the first 20 minutes, which he then showed to the producers before asking for more money to finish it off. The low-budget quickie had been turned into something bigger in Scott's hands, and was to make a star out of Sigourney Weaver and a lasting cinematic image out of Swiss artist H. R. Geiger's monster designs.

The resulting film, *Alien*, was the surprise hit of 1979 and launched Scott into the box-office big league. He went on to direct *Blade Runner* (1982) starring Harrison Ford, *Legend* (1986) with Tom Cruise, *Someone to Watch Over Me* (1987) and Michael Douglas and Andy Garcia in the dark thriller *Black Rain* (1989). *Thelma & Louise* (1991) was followed by the historic epic *1492: Conquest of Paradise*, again featuring Sigourney Weaver, and *White Squall* (1996).

'The main reason I chose to do this film,' said the 53-year-old Scott of *Thelma & Louise*, 'was that I've never done anything like it before. This is a film where the emphasis – the driving force, if you will – is almost totally on character, rather than where a spaceship comes from.'

Thelma & Louise is essentially a road movie – a hitherto almost exclusively male genre – featuring two gun-toting women on the run from the law. It was the story and the script that brought Ridley Scott to the project. 'Rarely do scripts come along that are about truth. This one most certainly is and it never deviates from that. It's humorous, it's dramatic, it's even slightly mythical in proportions. That's just about everything you can ask for from a really good story.'

The 'really good story' came from the pen of screenwriter Callie Khouri, a 33-year-old former music video producer. 'I got the idea while sitting in my car outside of my house one night,' recalled Khouri of the project's beginnings. 'What could possibly happen in the lives of two women, two best friends, that would force them to chose between what they had and what they might be able to have? What one event, what mistake perhaps, would make them journey out into the unknown? From there the story just started rolling out.'

The central characters in the drama are Thelma Dickson (Geena Davis), a suburban housewife, married to a male chauvinist pig, Darryl (Christopher McDonald). What Darryl fails to realise about his high school sweetheart, now his docile wife of many years, is that in reality she's had it with being docile. It just takes the right spark to set Thelma off on a course that changes everyone's lives forever.

That spark appears in the form of her best friend, Louise Sawyer (Susan Sarandon), a coffee shop waitress who is having trouble getting her current boyfriend Jimmy (Michael Madsen) to commit to their on-again, off-again relationship. The older of the pair, Louise is also fed up waiting around for her life to begin.

What the women decide they need is a weekend break away from the men in

Thelma & Louise was Brad Pitt's big break. He was only on screen for ten minutes, but his acting in the role of a charming and seductive crook was enough to make a lasting impression

Thelma (Geena Davis) does not realise that JD is more interested in
her money than her body, and is totally taken in by his good looks and easy manner.

their lives. Their aim is to give them some space to look at things, to get some
perspective on their current predicaments, but instead the trip turns into a journey
to hell and back. During a stop at a roadside bar in Arkansas, the two Texans run
into the kind of men they're trying to get away from. Shooting a would-be rapist, the
pair end up on the run from a likely murder charge, with the police – led by a
sympathetic Harvey Keitel - hot on their tails. Their on-the-road escapades –
including meeting Brad Pitt's charming rogue JD – make up the bulk of the movie.

Scriptwriter Khouri saw the film as an allegory, revealing truths and
generalisations about life, and not just a women's film. 'As a person, I truly believe
that you get more than one shot in life,' she said of her philosophy behind the film.
'Thelma and Louise's road trip is really a passage to some greater journey. As they
turn the corner of the highway, they take one more step toward a way of life they
never thought they could have - a life where they truly make their own decisions
and, in the end, are happier for it.'

Principal photography for *Thelma & Louise* began on Monday 11th June 1990

JD, Brad's character in *Thelma & Louise*, seduces Thelma (Geena Davis) in a
motel room. Brad was reported to be very nervous during shooting.

in a tree-lined residential area of Tarzana, California which was to feature in the
film's opening scenes as Thelma's small-town Arkansas neighbourhood. For six
weeks the production commandeered homes, businesses and public buildings all
around the Southern California area, including the Silver Bullet Saloon in Long
Beach, where 250 local extras performed a raucous country-western line dance
known as the 'Tush Push', and the famous DuPar's restaurant in Thousand Oaks,
which served as the coffee shop where Louise works as a waitress.

The company then moved to Bakersfield, where local oil fields and the lush
green crops of the San Joaquin Valley served as some of the roadside stops in
Oklahoma visited by the on-the-run pair.

During August the cast and crew, numbering about 175 in total, relocated to the
former uranium mining town of Moab, Utah. Situated on the banks of the Colorado
River, Moab is home to the majestic red rock formations of Arches National Park.
Much of south eastern Utah, including abandoned ghost towns like Cisco, was used
in the depiction of Arizona and New Mexico in the film.

'During pre-production for the film we travelled the exact route taken by the
characters in the film,' said Scott. They decided, however, that it was impractical to

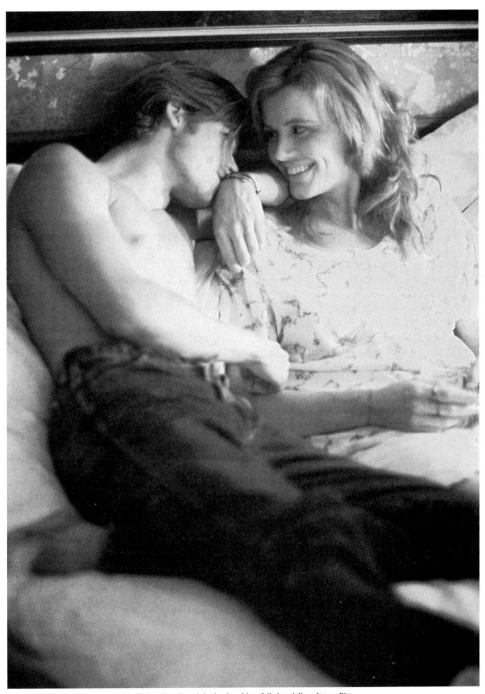

Thelma experienced the orgasm with JD that her chauvinist husband has failed to deliver. It was Pitt who dubbed it the "$6000" orgasm in reference to the money JD stole from her afterwards.

film on that route, despite the attractions of the scenery. 'Southern California and south eastern Utah each provided innumerable locations stemming from one particular base. Although we did shoot at many different sites, logistically speaking it would have been much more difficult to move from state-to-state.' Brad Pitt therefore did not have to travel too far from his home base in Los Angeles.

In the film Louise picks up her life savings from her boyfriend Jimmy. Her $6,700 looks like it'll be enough to see the pair safely on their way to Mexico. However, she didn't count on the sexual attraction the hitch-hiker they pick up would have for Thelma. His outlaw good looks and his tips on how to politely rob a small store bowl over Thelma. It isn't long before the couple tumble into bed in one of the most talked-about scenes in the whole movie. Thelma enjoys her first orgasm courtesy of JD, but she pays the price when the suave thief makes off with the money that she had been looking after for Louise. Pitt himself dubbed the scene 'the $6,000 orgasm'.

Filming the scene was not as easy or as much fun as the finished product looked on screen. *People* magazine reported one crew member recalling Pitt being very nervous. 'He was absolutely charming, very shy and very nervous. His biggest concern was that his mother wouldn't approve.' After all, he had to sweep the woman off her feet and make a big impression on the female audience in the cinema too, if the role was to be convincing. It was a tall order, but director Ridley Scott was sympathetic. 'Ridley would let us play around a lot,' said Pitt of the scene. 'He'd say, "Okay, we got that one. Let's try something else."' Once it was all cut together, the magic of the movies became apparent. What had taken hours to film and had seemed pretty silly, uncomfortable and embarrassing at the time, turned out to be convincing and charged with impact.

In fact, Pitt and Davis got on so well during the filming of that particular scene and on the film in general that rumours swept the set that they were enjoying a real-life liaison. Davis was in the process of separating from her then husband Jeff Goldblum (star of David Cronenberg's *The Fly*, and later a key character in Steven Spielberg's *Jurassic Park*) after five years, so could have been open to the opportunities offered. Maybe Davis was as swept off her feet as her character Thelma was in the film by Pitt's charisma and perfect physique.

Whatever the truth of these tales, Pitt was going to have problems living with the scene. 'I'm having trouble living up to that $6,000 orgasm,' Pitt confided to *Interview* magazine in 1992. 'I prefer to look at the film as about people in dead-end situations, and then an event puts them on a different path. They can become victims of that, or they can take control of it.'

Pitt knew that *Thelma & Louise* would be a good career move: 'I went after the part knowing it would bring me more opportunities.' Working with a cast including Geena Davis, Susan Sarandon and Harvey Keitel – all of whom he shared screen time with – couldn't fail to teach him something about the star business. 'They were fun and exciting,' said Pitt to London's *Guardian* newspaper about Davis and Sarandon. 'It's like when you play tennis with someone better than you – your game gets better.'

After half a decade of jobbing roles in Hollywood, Pitt was ready for the big time. 'I knew that part was going to come along. I can't explain it, but I knew it. Sometimes I was patient, and sometimes I was anxious, but I knew. And then, when it came along, I knew I was going to get it. I read it and immediately I knew. And I

Pondering the possible imminence of fame.

knew this guy to the end,' said Pitt of JD.

'I figured it would be a role like JD. It's something I'm good at – a Southern guy. It basically opened the door for some kind of respect, working with all those great people.'

Pitt was right – it was easy for him to play the role. JD was the type of guy he was familiar with, growing up in Missouri. A much more likeable character than Billy in *Too Young to Die?*, JD was nevertheless ruined Thelma and Louise's chance to get safely away from the authorities after them. He was seductive and smooth with Thelma, but more of his true cowardly and spineless character came through under interrogation by Harvey Keitel's pursuing cop.

Scott's film seemed to hit a raw nerve in American society and on its release it provoked acres of press coverage. Many critics attacked the film as anti-men in a controversy that rumbled in newspapers and magazines for weeks following the film's Memorial Day 1991 opening weekend.

Over those first four days the film took $6.1 million, low for a summer release, but a good performance for a relatively low budget film (set by *Variety* at $18.5 million) driven by two women stars. By the end of a month, the film had reached $23 million. The all-male star-driven *Backdraft* – the film that had gained the services of William Baldwin and allowed Brad Pitt to step into JD's jeans and cowboy boots – took $15.7 million on the same opening weekend, and the psychiatric comedy *What About Bob?* starring Richard Dreyfuss and Bill Murray took $11.3 million.

Under a headline asking 'Can *Thelma & Louise* continue to defy gravity?' Hollywood showbiz bible *Variety* saw the surprisingly high numbers of the opening weekend for such a small film as a sign of things to come. The picture looked set to take on the big studio blockbusters in the early summer of 1991, *Variety* putting its early success down to 'extraordinary reviews and word-of-mouth and the kind of media attention that turns a movie into a cultural phenomenon'.

Audiences were unusually vocal during the film, with women cheering when Louise fires off Thelma's .38, shooting the would-be rapist dead in the car park outside the roadside bar. Men in the audience may have found themselves uncomfortable with some of the points the film made against their sex, but as Susan Sarandon said, 'Only men who wear excessive gold jewellery are going to be intimidated by this film. It's not a feminist movie. These two women still talk about men and still want to be with them, just like Geena and me.'

The male-female 'sex war' issues were always in Ridley Scott's mind while making the film: 'It's two women moving through a landscape where they encounter men, all kinds of men - an uninterested husband, a Peter Pan-type boyfriend, a sensitive cop, a foul-mouthed trucker. This is where the film takes apart the whole male species - one total male being is inferred within the eight men in the film. That is not to say that this film is anti-male or bashes men by any means. It's just an example to show that women are definitely the more vulnerable of the species, not physically or mentally, but emotionally.'

Everyone weighed in with their views on the film, from psychologists, sexologists, academics and countless lesser pundits. Los Angeles critic Sheila Benson accused the people behind the film of betraying responsible feminists by promoting revenge, sadism and the denigration of men. For every critic who wrote

Brad can play smooth and seductive or lost and vulnerable.

of 'female fascism', another hailed the movie as a 'feminist manifesto'. The edition of *Time* magazine which devoted its cover to *Thelma & Louise* trailed its coverage by claiming: 'A white hot debate rages over whether *Thelma & Louise* celebrates liberated females, male bashers - or outlaws.'

The New York Daily News found the film 'degrading to men, with pathetic stereotypes of testosterone-crazed behaviour. It justifies armed robbery, manslaughter and chronic drunken-driving as exercises in consciousness raising.' Another critic, John Leo in the *US News and World Report*, complained of 'an explicit fascist theme, wedded to the bleakest form of feminism, buried shallowly in a genuinely funny buddy movie'. *The Los Angeles Times* saw the movie as 'a sisterhood-bash-a-thon'. Defenders of the film included prominent critics like Janet Maslin in *The New York Times* and Terence Rafferty of *The New Yorker*, who called the film 'a crazily over-stuffed Hollywood entertainment'.

The stars were equally happy about the furore that greeted their work. Criticism that the men in the movie were clichéd and derisory was met by Geena Davis's argument that the positive portrayal of the women characters was a departure as far as Hollywood films were concerned. 'Ninety-nine percent of movies are like: kill the women, slice them open, blow their heads off,' Davis told *The Evening Standard*. 'All Hollywood movies are about letting women be naked, or raped, or abused. The exhilarating thing about *Thelma & Louise* is that you realise you can change your life and get your own power.'

Susan Sarandon took a lighter view of the film. 'We've got this strange effect of having this women's *Odd Couple* in *Mad Max* country.'

Brad Pitt didn't escape the controversy either, with his views on the morality of the film also being solicited. 'I don't think the movie has some big moral the way a lot of people are making out,' he told *The New York Times*. 'I don't find it controversial.'

Controversial the film certainly was, and in among all the hoo-haa, the reviews occasionally found room to pick out Brad Pitt's performance for a special mention. Terrence Rafferty in *The New Yorker* was one. 'Brad Pitt has the sullen handsomeness – and the white cowboy hat – of the country singer Dwight Yoakim.'

The Village Voice's J. Hoberman noted: 'Thelma falls for a boyish hold-up man (Brad Pitt) who, among other things, teaches her robbery etiquette.' *Rolling Stone* threw in it's tuppence worth, too, on the character of JD: 'a hitchhiking hunk charmingly played by Brad Pitt'.

The final word on the film and the controversy surrounding it should be *Variety*'s: 'Despite some delectably funny scenes between the sexes, Ridley Scott's pic isn't about women vs men. It's about freedom, like any good road picture. In that sense, and in many others, it's a classic.' The film went on to win an Oscar for Best Original Screenplay the following March.

At last Brad Pitt stood out from all the other pretty boys of Hollywood, the would-be stars and wannabe heart-throbs. Coverage moved quickly from the film reviews and 'controversy' articles to the pages of the teen magazines. Features on him began appearing regularly, taking the actor by surprise. He'd had a brief taste of this before, when he'd appeared as the hunk of the month in *Dallas*, but he was quite unprepared for the teenage enthusiasm that goes with idol worship.

Juliette Lewis felt the full brunt of her boyfriend's new found stardom when they attended the official premiere of *Thelma & Louise*. 'Everyone was screaming

"Brad! Brad! Over here!" The flashbulbs are exploding in your face. It was like a brainwashing trip,' she recalled, as the effect of the movie on Pitt's profile began to sink in.

Rather than cash in on his new found fame, Pitt refused to play the JD clones that the scripts starting to land on his doorstep required of him. He'd played the part twice before – in *The Image*, where he dressed and acted almost exactly as he was to do in *Thelma & Louise*, and to an extent in the character of Billy in *Too Young to Die?*, although that performance was more like a prototype of Early Grayce from *Kalifornia*. For his next role, he was determined to find something very different.

The Favor was inappropriately titled insofar as Brad's career was concerned, although he did make the most of the poor material.

Before the impact of *Thelma & Louise* was felt by the movie-going public, the word about Brad Pitt had spread through the Hollywood grapevine, and it wasn't long before he was back in front of the cameras, in another role which, despite his best career intentions, capitalised on his sex appeal.

Although made in 1991, *The Favor* didn't get a cinema release, caught up in the problems that plagued producers Orion, Woody Allen's old studio, when bankruptcy loomed. The film was shelved, only to be belated released on video in 1994, mainly on the strength of Brad Pitt's by-then growing star status.

Pitt was cast again in the role of a boyfriend, but with the sex appeal of his *Thelma & Louise* character mixed in. *The Favor* was an ensemble comedy piece about love and romance in the 90s, written by Josann McGibbon and Sara Parriot, and directed by Donald Petrie.

The film focused on the romantic entanglements of four characters. Pitt played Elliot Fowler, a young and successful Portland artist who is enjoying a fulfilling affair with gallery owner Emily, played by Elizabeth McGovern. The pair are friends with a married couple, Kathy and Peter (played by Harley Jane Kozak and Bill Pullman), who seem happy with their routine lives and two kids. Emily discovers, however, that Kathy can't forget about an old school friend that she was infatuated with, but never actually slept with, and has been fantasising about him in anticipation of an upcoming 15th anniversary school reunion. He now lives in Denver, where Emily is about to go on a trip - without Pitt's Elliott because of a fight they have had at a birthday party. Unlikely as it may seem, Kathy manages to persuade Emily to look up her old would-be boyfriend and sleep with him to satisfy her overwhelming curiosity – the 'favor' of the title. Surprisingly, the cast almost

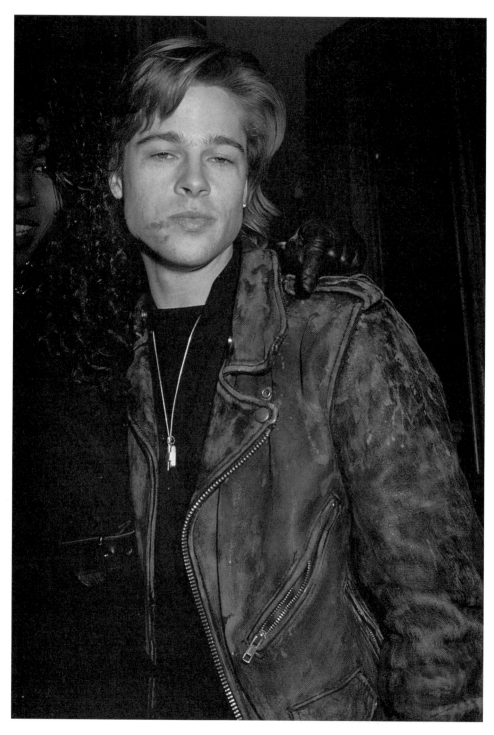

managed to pull off this silly story with straight faces.

Upon returning to Elliott after her fling on the side for her friend, Emily finds herself pregnant, and unsure of who the father might be. Further complications ensue, and things are finally resolved with another trip to Denver for all the major characters.

Bill Pullman probably comes off best in the cast, playing a academic computer science nerd who becomes worried that his wife is having an affair with Pitt. Tom, the object of Kathy's fantasies, was played by Ken Wahl, star of the 80s cult TV series *Wiseguy*.

Pitt did his best with the thin material he had to work with. His character is first seen in bed with McGovern, referencing his *Thelma & Louise* star turn, before he tries to sketch her - based on Pitt's real-life habit.

Pitt had tried comedy before, in some of his TV roles and in *Happy Together*. It was something he felt he should be able to do successfully, but all his comedy film roles failed dismally. Doing *The Favor* was a useful lesson – concentrate on the straight dramatics and forget about going for laughs.

Certainly, the few reviews the film had were enough to hammer home the message to the cast. *People* wrote 'The Favor cannot lay claim to a single plot twist that is at all new or interestingly redone. The cast members, particularly Pullman and Pitt, deserve an audience's deepest, deepest sympathy.'

In the film Pitt does manage to hold his own in a thankless role against experienced performers like McGovern and Pullman. Lightly funny, but ultimately inconsequential, *The Favor* doesn't amount to much as a film and is even less successful as a follow-up to Pitt's breakthrough role in *Thelma & Louise*. As far as Pitt was concerned, *The Favor* could have stayed on the distributors shelf indefinitely.

While Pitt was having his first taste of what it was like to be a real hot property, living with Juliette Lewis gave him a solid base in the weird world of Los Angeles. The pair were devoted to developing their careers, and Lewis, with *Cape Fear*, was rapidly catching up with Pitt in the fame game. With talk of possible Oscar nominations for Lewis, features in major magazines and all the coverage given to Pitt in *Thelma & Louise*, the pair couldn't be happier. There was trouble ahead for them, however, but at the beginning of the 90s they set about enjoying their hard-won success.

For Pitt the problem of keeping his career on the right track after the impact of *Thelma & Louise* was paramount. He'd made a turkey with *The Favor* - but no one was going to see that for a while, giving him time to carve out a niche for himself in distinctive roles. Just such a role was right around the corner in the cult movie *Johnny Suede*. Now it was up to him to turn his 15 minutes of fame into a lasting career.

Hollywood's newest hot property smoulders.

JOHNNY SUEDE

6 The Cool World of Johnny Suede

BRAD PITT's first top-billed, starring role was in a low-budget character piece to be helmed by a first-time film director.

Most actors in his position would have milked the notoriety he'd gained from his brief fling with Geena Davis in Ridley Scott's controversial film for all it was worth. But Pitt had other concerns. He wanted the fame and fortune that being a star could offer him, but he also wanted to stretch himself a bit. The title role in *Johnny Suede* was to be the first film to give Hollywood's newest rising star that chance.

From the beginning, director Tom DiCillo's film *Johnny Suede* had all the elements to make it an instant cult classic. DiCillo himself had previously been a director of photography, working on such low-budget, independent cult films as Jim Jarmusch's *Stranger Than Paradise*. He came from a theatre background, where he'd acted and directed, and it was in the New York acting classes he'd attended that DiCillo had first generated the character of Johnny Suede.

DiCillo came up with his offbeat hero as an antidote to all the run-of-the-mill stuff his fellow students were doing to hone their acting skills. 'Day after day they brought in pieces *à la* Tennessee Williams or Eugene O'Neill, so I said, bullshit! I'm going to come in tomorrow and just start talking, and they're not going to know whether what I'm saying just happened to me, or whether I wrote it.'

'I did a guy who appears to have got everything together, but really hasn't, who keeps stumbling every step of the way. It seemed an interesting sort of hero – the exact opposite to Woody Allen, who I find boring after two minutes.'

His off-the-cuff character went down well enough for DiCillo to invest time and effort developing it further. He eventually came up with enough material to launch a one-man show, all from his initial ten-minute monologue. 'It was immediately accessible to do on stage – it was cheap! My one-man show I mounted for about $3000, way off Broadway!'

DiCillo eventually found his way onto New York University's film-making course, where he struck up a friendship with Jim Jarmusch. 'We were in the same class together at film school and I was assigned, completely arbitrarily, to shoot a student film for him. That led to my shooting *Permanent Vacation* in 1981. That led to me shooting two more films with him after we graduated – at times it was an alternative to painting apartments!'

DiCillo found himself going down a career path he didn't intend, and it took some effort to give it up to strike out in a new direction – making his own movies rather than being known for shooting someone else's. After all, why give away all his good ideas to others?' 'I never studied cinematography and had never planned to,' said DiCillo, 'I guess it was just my eye. I shot *Stranger Than Paradise* [which won Jarmusch the Camera D'Or at Cannes in 1984]. I found myself going down this road that I didn't want to be on. Eventually it became depressing because it created a category for me as a cameraman which is not what I wanted to do. I spent a long time out of the business totally, until finally everything came together for me to make *Johnny Suede*.'

'Brad Pitt plays the sweet, dim pompadoured hero with a charisma that reminds me...of James Dean." (*Financial Times*)

61

For his film DiCillo returned to his original one man show, which had been entitled 'Johnny Suede: Lessons in Love'. The original play had been extremely sexist, a factor that had worried DiCillo prior to performing it. 'My biggest fear was that some woman in the audience would stand up and yell at me "You arsehole!" but they didn't - they found it fascinating. That's what encouraged me to write the screenplay.'

DiCillo had some help in developing his script from an unexpected source - the actor Robert Redford. Redford had set up the Sundance Institute, an organisation based around the annual Sundance Film Festival of independent films with the aim of promoting independent, non-studio film production in America. Promoting new talent was a major aim. 'The script was invited to the Sundance Institute,' recalls DiCillo. 'They paid for me to stay there two weeks and film some scenes from it. For all its faults, Sundance is the only place in America where they allow you to genuinely play around. That's one of the most important, creative things you can do, to say, I'm gonna try this...whoops, I just fell flat on my face in front of 100 people. And then to try again.'

With a script ready to go, the next task facing the neophyte director was finding the funding for his film. 'I hit everyone I knew for money, but it was always a dead end street. I probably had the worst experience a first-time director could have with financing.' The National Endowment for the Arts came to his rescue, kicking in $25,000, which attracted the rest of the finance he needed. 'The money came from a Swiss producer who liked the script and the fact that it was not much money - $500,000. I had intentionally kept the locations simple, mostly interiors. It has basically the same structure as the play, though it is an expansion.'

As with the stage version, DiCillo was keen to play the lead character of Johnny himself, as well as writing and directing the film - a real Orson Welles-style debut. He thought better of it, however, deciding to cast someone else in the role - but it had to be an actor who wasn't too well known and who would not bring any baggage from any other roles.

He first tried auditioning in New York, a process DiCillo found fruitless: 'All these guys coming in and acting goofy,' was his pithy account of the process. He switched to Los Angeles, where pickings were richer. However, he still wasn't finding what he was looking for in those who auditioned. 'It was unbelievable how many "hot" young American actors missed the point of what the part was about. I wanted an unknown, and I was looking, I realised, for someone a bit like Jon Voight in *Midnight Cowboy* – innocent and a bit stupid, but not Latin, not ethnic. From Middle America.'

Onto the scene came someone who looked interesting from his picture. Brad Pitt had on his CV an as-yet-unreleased film called *Thelma & Louise*, and DiCillo had never seen the young actor in action. 'Brad Pitt came in, a bit nervous, very Southern,' recalled DiCillo. 'I asked him to do Johnny's monologue about suede – "rough but soft, strong but quiet" – and he took off his cowboy boot, looked at it with love, and spoke with that gentle quality which showed he understood that, underneath, the character is absolutely terrified. He'd got it just right.'

DiCillo was impressed by Pitt's ability, out of all those actors who had played before him, to get right to the heart of the character. He had found an actor on the right wavelength able to pull off the character in the script and bring him to life on the screen. 'Brad was the only one that showed that this love for this shoe he was

Brad's portrayal of the fundamental innocence of Johnny Suede's fifties-obsessed romantic helped the film achieve cult status.

holding was genuine and came from a fear and insecurity in himself: that he had to love this shoe, because he had no other identity without it.'

For Brad Pitt the role of *Johnny Suede* was ideal. It allowed him to build on his *Thelma & Louise* teen idol credentials without simply repeating the young stud stunt. Instead here was a really different character, a unique soul and he was the perfect person to play the part. 'I want to keep the work interesting,' Pitt said.

There were other attractions in the part. The fact that Johnny Suede was an aspiring musician appealed to the actor who'd shelved any musical ambition he may have been nurturing. There were other, deeper, reasons for taking the role. Without knowing it, DiCillo had in his personal creation come up with a character that shared a lot of basic similarities with Pitt in real life. 'It's almost about self-discovery,' Pitt told Alison Powell in *Interview* magazine. 'You know, how you try to emulate this or that, and then you wake up one morning and realise what an idiot you've been?'

At its heart, *Johnny Suede* is a romance, even if it's a little twisted and off-the-wall. Suede, not so much played but incarnated by Pitt, is a huge Ricky Nelson fan who sports a gravity-defying pompadour. He has an image, with his 50s cool chic and his black suede shoes. Although seemingly contemporary and filmed in out-of-the-way New York locations, the film could be timeless and set in any grim American metropolis. Johnny gains his suede shoes as if they were gifts from the Gods when they fall out of the sky one day. Believing this means his success as a rock star is assured Suede deludes himself, as he does in his relationship with girlfriend Darlette (Alison Moir). Convinced he's a great musician and an even better lover, Suede is spectacularly incompetent in both departments. What he does boast is an overwhelming sense of bravado and an unbelievable innocence that seems to carry

Johnny Suede and the woman he meets in an alley (Cheryl Costa).

him through most situations unscathed.

The shoes from heaven are his reward for rescuing a woman from a seeming gang-rape as the film opens. They complete his outfit, his all-important image. The rest of the film is a series of picaresque adventures, during which Darlette dumps Johnny, returning to her ex-boyfriend, a violent photographer curiously named Flip Doubt. Soon, Johnny has a new, if unlikely, girlfriend in the form of Yvonne (Catherine Keener). She is more down-to-earth than any other character in the film and she manages to drag Johnny kicking and screaming to some sense of reality by tossing away his beloved black suede shoes.

'There's something humorous about someone who believes so strongly in his own self-image,' said DiCillo of the character he created. 'An identity drops on Johnny's head like the suede shoes - an identity that fits him perfectly. I was fascinated to start peeling back those layers. I see *Johnny Suede* as a kind of art comedy about a man's slight glimpse of himself.'

Hardly strong on plot, DiCillio's debut film was certainly strong on style. Saturated in colour and boasting stylised performances from all the principals, *Johnny Suede* became an immediate cult success. Getting there wasn't easy, though, as the making of the film was no bed of roses.

Brad Pitt was a leading man on a film at last, and he intended to make the most of his situation and the power that came with it. That flexing of his star muscle was to bring him into conflict with the writer-director. 'The making of *Johnny Suede* was a very long, detailed process. It wasn't peaches and cream. I didn't want any fucking ad-libbing,' said DiCillo of his leading man. 'If you ad-lib words like "Hey, you know?" and "Got me?", it doesn't work. I said, "Brad - just say the words."'

Pitt's sin – after winning the part by standing out at the auditions because he displayed a strong understanding of the role – was to play the part too literally in 50s style, throwing in then-hip catchphrases not in the script. His approach showed an actor still unsure of his craft, unwilling to trust wholly to the script or the director. He was beginning to become convinced of his own star potential. Being a prima donna on the set was not to gain him many friends.

DiCillo was to gain his revenge three years later in 1995 in his second film *Living in Oblivion*. A clever and witty comedy set behind the scenes of the production of a low-budget film, *Living in Oblivion* starred Steve Buscemi as a frustrated director and James LeGros as a prima donna film star named Chad Palomino. Palomino is forever throwing tantrums and tossing his tuppence worth into the creative process. Calling LeGros the 'Brad Pitt of independents', *People* magazine asked: 'Are the rumours true that LeGros' no-brains pretty boy actor is actually based on Pitt?'

LeGros said: 'Chad's an amalgam of different actors I've worked with – three in particular, who shall remain nameless. Brad's a handsome devil ... ' He denied that the part was a send up of Brad Pitt, while Pitt himself claimed he wanted to play the role in *Living in Oblivion* with his *Johnny Suede* director, but couldn't due to other commitments.

Whatever the on-set friction between the rising star leading man and the frustrated independent director, DiCillo still believed that Pitt was the only actor capable of bringing *Johnny Suede* to life the way he envisaged the character. He had other reasons to be grateful for Pitt's participation. As the filming was completed, *Thelma & Louise* was released and Pitt's star had arrived.

Brad Pitt, in Johnny Suede pompadour, discusses his role with director Tom DiCillo. The pair had different views of the way the part should be played.

'Miramax bought the US rights to the film without even seeing it, based on three things,' said DiCillo. 'We'd just won the first prize at the Locarno Festival [the Golden Leopard award], it had got a great review in *Variety* and it starred Brad Pitt.'   However, signs of director–star jealousies remained in DiCillo's complaint about the film's distribution. 'Miramax is now trying to capitalise on Brad,' he said when the *Thelma & Louise* controversies were in full swing, 'which is a little annoying – I would like them to create an identity for the film too...'

Pitt was keen to credit the limited success of *Johnny Suede* to Tom DiCillo: 'That film was all DiCillo. Someone should cut open his head and lay it out. I think it would be very entertaining. *Days of Thunder* it ain't! There will be a group of people out there who will appreciate it. I want to try a wide variety of things before I get stuck in some corner. I want to show what I can do. I've got big plans, big goals,' announced Pitt, aware that his time had now come.

Pitt's Baptist parents turned out to be the biggest critics of *Johnny Suede*. 'I like it,' Pitt told Britain's *Empire* magazine, 'but my folks hated it. I always know. I talked to them on the phone and they said, "We're going to rent *Johnny Suede* tonight" – these movies don't make it to where I grew up. And a month went by and I realised they hadn't mentioned it...' Later, in another phone call Pitt's grandfather told him he'd finally seen *Johnny Suede*: 'We saw that movie of yours. Betty? What was the name of that movie we didn't like...?'

The reviews were kinder than Pitt's own family. The *Variety* review – one of the three factors that sold the movie sight unseen to Miramax for American distribution – was particularly good. 'Brad Pitt, fresh from stealing scenes in *Thelma & Louise*, gives Johnny the right kind of innocent appeal, and the rest of the cast surround him with loving care,' read the write-up.

In *The Village Voice*, J. Hoberman pointed out the cult film's most successful feature: 'It is DiCillo's good fortune to have Brad Pitt play his sincerely self-absorbed hero. Indeed, for a stylish exercise in cool, *Johnny Suede* is extremely well acted. *Johnny Suede* may look like a cartoon, but it is deep enough to leave open questions...'

Upon the film's British release in June 1992, the critics were also quick to claim Pitt as a new cinema icon in the making. David Robinson in *The Times* called Pitt 'a striking young actor, [who] effectively catches Johnny's absurdity, dumb cunning and unselfconscious sensuality.' Derek Malcolm in *The Guardian* saw versatility in Pitt's first leading man performance. 'Pitt's slow burn performance – totally different from his portrait of the ne'er-do-well lover in *Thelma & Louise* – is memorable because he never camps it up too much.'

Alexander Walker in *The London Evening Standard* joined many who picked up on Pitt's *Thelma & Louise* notoriety before predicting big things for the actor. 'Pitt is a personable performer. He has the romantic-loner look of James Dean. Rediscover Brad Pitt before his face is everywhere.'

The Financial Times film critic made the same comparison: 'Brad Pitt plays the sweet, dim pompadoured hero with a charisma that reminds me - indeed has reminded everyone to judge by the American press quotes - of James Dean.'

The inevitable James Dean comparison had risen again. Brad Pitt had played pastiche Dean in his *Tales From the Crypt* episode, and he was touted alongside other young actors as the 'new James Dean'. 'I don't think about it much,' said Pitt, then aged 27, three years older than Dean when he died. 'They have to compare you to something at the beginning, but I'll prove myself on my own terms as I go along. Don't get me wrong - it's a very nice compliment.' The 'compliment' was made so often after *Johnny Suede*, that Pitt began to tire of it, especially when asked if his Dean resemblance was deliberate. 'Why would anyone pattern themselves after a dead person?' he once snapped at a reporter who made the suggestion.

The combined press coverage of *Thelma & Louise* and *Johnny Suede* did go to Brad Pitt's head, though. *Johnny Suede* was not to be the last time that Pitt would have clashes on film sets with directors and co-stars. Both *Legends of the Fall* and *Interview with the Vampire* would become subject to Pitt's egotistic demands.

The Village Voice film critic may have compared *Johnny Suede* to a cartoon because of its hyper-reality, but Pitt was next to star in a real cartoon-live action hybrid, director Ralph Bakshi's *Cool World*.

A controversial Hollywood figure, Ralph Bakshi was the maverick cartoon genius behind the animated X-rated *Fritz the Cat* (1972), as well as other animated features like *Wizards* (1977), *American Pop* (1981) and an unfinished version of J.R.R. Tolkein's lavish epic fantasy *The Lord of the Rings* (1978).

Cool World started development two years before Bakshi began serious shooting in May 1991 in a meeting he had with producer Frank Mancuso Jr.

Mancuso had produced the *Friday the 13th* films as well as the thriller *Internal Affairs* (1990), starring Richard Gere. The two men discussed a project about a man who becomes trapped in a cartoon world he created. Bakshi suggested combining live action with animation as a way to tell the story.

Development began on this reverse version of *Who Framed Roger Rabbit?* (1988) with Bakshi expecting the project to be his most technically challenging effort. His previous animated features had all tested the limits of techniques and technology and he saw *Cool World* as a chance to do the same. He was also itching to get back to film-making after an eight-year hiatus during which he'd studied painting.

The film would require a brave team of actors who would be willing to act opposite characters who were not there in the studio, but would be added by a team of animators afterwards. The first star to be attracted to the project was Kim Basinger, interested in the role of Holli Would, a cartoon character who longs to become human. 'Holli's a great girl,' said Bakshi of his creation. 'She wants more than she has. She wants to be real, which is admirable, and she does everything she

Playing opposite Gabriel Byrne as the cartoonist Jack Deebs in *Cool World* was lot easier than shooting scenes with absent animated characters who would be added later.

can to become real. She's a girl who wants to get the hell out of where she is – and there are girls like that in Brooklyn [where Bakshi grew up] that want to get out and go to LA.'

It was clear from early sketches of the character that Bakshi and his animators were already basing Holli on Basinger well before she showed interest. Having starred in the Sean Connery 1983 Bond comeback movie *Never Say Never Again* (1983) and in the steamy *9 1/2 Weeks* (1986) opposite Mickey Rourke, Basinger had featured in *Batman* (1989), *Final Analysis* (1992), *The Marrying Man* (1991) and *The Getaway* (1994), the last two opposite her husband Alec Baldwin. Producer Mancuso believed the production enjoyed a stroke of luck in actually managing to secure her for the role. Booking her immediately raised both the profile and the budget of the project. What was originally intended as a low-budget version of *Who Framed Roger Rabbit?* was now on its way to summer blockbuster territory.

The cartoonist who creates the animated *Cool World* of the title was played by Gabriel Byrne, an Irish actor who was best known to American audiences for his gangster role in the Coen Brothers' film *Miller's Crossing* (1990), and later for his part as one of *The Usual Suspects* (1995). Byrne described his character, Jack Deebs, as a conjuror who has brought his deepest fears to life. 'It's a real journey for him,' he said of Deebs's trip into the animated domain, 'with a beginning place to an end place and he really doesn't know where he's going.'

The film follows Deebs as he experiences his life unhinging when he finds himself in the two-dimensional world he created. Holli Would is one of the characters he encounters; she is a doodle who has sprung fully formed from his mind, and she desperately wants to be human. The only way the cartoon characters can become real is by having sex with a real human – a typically adult twist from Ralph Bakshi.

The only other human to have entered *Cool World* is detective Frank Harris, the part played by Brad Pitt. A tortured young victim of a tragedy, Harris is a World War Two veteran who seeks solace in the animated world to which he has escaped.

'Harris took some hard knocks in life, so he checked out,' said Brad Pitt of his troubled character. 'Now he's here in *Cool World* and it's really grand here. It's fantasy time.'

Because of his performance in *Thelma & Louise*, Pitt was the actor that Frank Mancuso wanted for the unusual role. 'Harris is one of the most complex characters of *Cool World*. He stayed in *Cool World* because he was frightened [of the real world]. Now he's stuck in an unreal world.'

Ralph Bakshi was attracted to the project because of its potential for groundbreaking animation work and because of its semi-adult approach to animation, not surprising considering *Fritz the Cat*. 'Animation for too long was basically just for children, and I think that was its biggest drawback. Not that children's films weren't beautiful, just that animation can do more. So this film represents the outer limits of animation.'

The tone of the script was difficult for Bakshi to define. 'There are three or four genres running through it,' he admitted. 'It has horror moments, it has *film noir* detective pulp moments, and it has pure cartoon moments.' Moreover, while Deebs is a contemporary character, Pitt's detective Harris sports 40s suits and spouts post-war lingo.

In *Cool World* Brad's Detective Frank Harris is one of two people who enter a cartoon world populated by doodles who want to become human.

The major problems were technical – how to combine the live action and animation elements successfully on a tight $16 million budget. For a solution Bakshi went back in time, to 1937 when the Disney studio developed the multi-plane camera, which mounts layers of artwork on glass plates, giving a 3D style depth-of-vision. This allowed the drawn backgrounds for the animation to also be used for the life-size live action sets.

'Economically, it was impossible for us to construct huge sets in the traditional manner,' said Bakshi. 'I came up with the idea of blowing up the animated backgrounds as photographs and constructing these to form the sets. We have turned the entire set into a live action multi-plane camera – a concept which is bound only by the size of the stage.' This breakthrough allowed the film to be produced cheaply and gave a bizarrely surreal 3D look to the 'real world' scenes.

Principal photography began with three weeks in the larger-than-life city of Las Vegas for all the live-action sequences and as the setting for the 'real world' portions of the film. Las Vegas was also the basis for the *Cool World* fantasy land.

'There is no better place in the world to serve as a cartoon city,' said Mancuso. An additional six weeks of shooting took place on soundstages in and around Los Angeles.

A specially designed facility was needed to accommodate the new animation technology being used. Bakshi hired a mix of veteran animators and newcomers, some of whom were still on their studies at the California Institute of the Arts. It took two months to complete a final edit of the live action material which was to be combined with the animation elements, a process which took a further nine months work by over 300 background artists, technicians, editors and animators. It was touch and go for the film to meet its scheduled opening date of July 1992.

The pressure on the stars, director and producer was great. The concept of *Cool World* was a difficult one to communicate to studio heads and publicists, never mind actually successfully pull off in the film itself. In the end, the project seems to have become too large for its individual elements to add up to something that made much sense.

'There's no question that this is a movie that's causing Ralph and me to stretch to places we've never been to before,' Mancuso admitted to science fiction TV and movie magazine *Starlog*. 'Ralph has never done live action before, and I've never been involved in animation. It has been taxing and, in a sense, alienating.'

The producer and director were not the only ones alienated from the production. The actors were having trouble coping with the unreality of what they were doing, with experienced film stars like Basinger and Byrne adrift from their normal reference points. The experience wasn't as bad for Pitt, who was just setting out on his cinematic adventures and was still open to new ways of working, but when asked about 'blue screen' work after the production his response was concise: 'Never again'.

Within the production staff it often seemed as though the right hand didn't know what the left hand was doing, resulting in a bizarre hodge-podge in the final film. Production designer Michael Corenblith was landed with the job of trying to knit the bits together into something that seemed consistent. 'We've drawn on a far broader range of comics, cartoons and contemporary art styles than we normally would,' he confessed to *Starlog*. 'We're dealing with so many different factions who each have their own method of doing things. I spend a lot of my time as a negotiator between the animators and illustrators. I make sure that both sides don't forget that there is a live-action movie going on here – and that things have to be created to a precise scale to accommodate live actors and stunts.'

The major problem with *Cool World* was precisely that the production seemed to loose sight of the human element. The actors – Basinger, Byrne and Pitt – simply became extra elements to be moved around in the mix. Bakshi seemed to miss his first opportunity to direct real actors. As it was, it was left up to the actors themselves to come up with characterisations. Pitt had more to work with than the others in his character and seemed to come off best in the film, but the entire project seems to have been doomed to be a brave experimental failure rather than a mainstream *Roger Rabbit*-style popular hit.

Paramount's marketing department was faced with the unforgiving task of selling the confused and confusing film to the movie-going public. They had an asset in Kim Basinger, as well as Pitt's rising star to hang the film on, but found the concept of cartoons who become real and humans hiding in cartoon worlds too complex to get across easily.

Someone, however, came up with the bright idea of draping the famous Hollywood landmark sign with a 75ft likeness of the *Cool World* cartoon Kim Basinger as a promotional gimmick. Receiving the odd request from Paramount to pop Kim Basinger's animated counterpart atop the letter 'D', the Parks Department agreed as Paramount was the only Hollywood film studio still actually located in the Hollywood area, the others having long since relocated to other parts of Los Angeles. Paramount didn't have to pay for the privilege, but they did make a donation of $27,000 to the sign maintenance fund and paid a further $27,000 to the post-1991 LA riots fund, Rebuild LA, as well as footing the bill for a two-man 24-hour guard.

The plan was not to the liking of the Hollywood Home-owners Association, who went to court to try and stop Paramount from pulling off their stunt. 'Los Angeles is the only city in the world that would take its most prominent monument and turn it into a common billboard,' complained Chuck Welch, president of the Association. 'I don't think you can rent the Eiffel Tower for a billboard, or the Tower of London, or the Washington Monument...'

The Association failed in its campaign and Paramount won millions of pounds worth of free publicity. It was all to no avail, however. The film still flopped, although it enjoys a healthy cult life on video – just like *Johnny Suede* before it. As for the Hollywood sign, it would appear that Paramount are destined to be the first and last organisation to get to tamper with its letters.

Released in July, *Cool World* suffered dismal reviews in both the United States and Europe. *The Village Voice* tried to outline some of the film's problems, laying the blame firmly at Bakshi's feet. 'He directs the badly synched actors so poorly,' wrote James Hannaham, 'that they pale against his crazed animated methadone clinic of wired wolfhounds, screaming telephones and cute yet megalomaniac bunnies.' Although clearly struggling with the material, Pitt came in for particular criticism from the *Voice*: 'Brad Pitt fails in every world suggested by the film...his performance is uncomfortable and mush-mouthed...'

Having boosted Pitt's career and per-film asking price with its glowing review of *Johnny Suede*, *Variety* was merciless in panning *Cool World*. Again, Hollywood animation rebel Ralph Bakshi was the main target. *Variety* called the film 'an ordeal...in the form of trial by animation. Bakshi has let his imagination run wild with almost brutal vigour, resulting in a guerrilla-like sensual assault unchecked by any traditional rules of storytelling.' Put more simply, in the words of *The New York Daily News*: 'Bakshi's skill as an animator continues to outshine his judgement about subject matter.'

In Britain the film fared a little better, with critics being kinder about Brad Pitt's role. *Sight and Sound* regarded him as the sole redeeming feature of the piece: 'The opening sequence, in which Brad Pitt as Frank suffers a motorbike accident, is the only well-directed live-action segment, while the *Cool World* sections are swamped by numerous irrelevant characters running or flying across the screen. Pitt and Gabriel Byrne struggle against the odds, though, unfortunately, the same cannot be said of Kim Basinger,' wrote critic Jeremy Clarke.

With many critics comparing *Cool World* unfavourably with *Who Framed Roger Rabbit?* and drawing comparisons (again unfavourably) between the Kathleen Turner-voiced Jessica Rabbit and Basinger's turn as Holli Would, *Cool*

World was on a hiding to nothing, despite its seasonal Christmas 1992 UK release.

Recalling that some of his family had not liked *Johnny Suede* much, Pitt was not too surprised to their unanimous reaction to *Cool World*. 'They all hated that one,' he recalled. 'It was dog shit, wasn't it? I like bad movies, 'cause I like to yell at the screen at home,' he joked.

In reality, though, starring in a flop was a bad experience. Quite apart from seeing a lot of invested time and effort go to waste as a film fails, it's not something that actors can easily recover from. 'I had my fears,' said Pitt of the troubled production. 'I wanted to see it, to see what went wrong, not like it's a big surprise. You see, the studio [Paramount] toned the script down because they wanted a PG, and in doing so they left all these holes. And of course new studio heads came in. They're not to blame, but if there was a chance to improve the film, they sure didn't take it. There's politics involved, which to me is the craziest thing, because it's anti-art. Ralph's too good a person, and it makes me mad.'

Pitt found himself on something of a personal and professional plateau in the early 90s. He'd suffered two mainstream flops in a row with *Johnny Suede* and *Cool World*, and it was a losing streak the actor couldn't afford to maintain. His bankability – and so his castability – would suffer if his next film failed. The search was on for a suitable property to give him the next boost up the Hollywood ladder.

His life had become far more complicated than it had been before, but in his laid-back, spaced-out way Pitt was coping. 'I honestly see things as very simple,' he said. 'When things get out of hand there's a simple answer. Some people are good at finding it quickly, some never find it.'

Despite the flops, he was famous, and was intent on enjoying his fame. 'I'm not surprised,' he told *Interview* magazine about his success; after all he'd worked for it. 'A whole lot of new steps come with it.' He was now in a position to sit back, during 1992, and mull over his feelings about Hollywood. 'This place has been good to me, but everyone makes judgements about it from afar. There are people, including me, who thought happiness was the place. This is why I left Missouri. I've found happiness is a way of travel.'

All was not perfect, however, in his private life. Pitt and Juliette Lewis had been spending a lot of time apart, pursuing their individual film careers. And the distance was putting pressure on the relationship.

7 The Road to Stardom

BY THE beginning of 1992 Pitt had already come a long way with what had seemed to be very little actual effort on his part. 'I've had it too easy,' he later admitted in a 1995 *Vanity Fair* interview. 'I'm starting to believe that anyone who's successful in these little circles has got to feel that way. That's why a lot of them don't survive it. You know, people want to be famous, but you have no idea what you're getting into. It just happens and the happening is big.'

The big break on *Thelma & Louise* had made him a recognised name and face in Hollywood. *The Favor* had done him a favour by vanishing, and he'd stuck to his guns by not simply repeating the JD role in a string of sex-themed movies, despite being offered many opportunities: 'Right now I have to prove there's more here than a pretty face, that there's substance,' he claimed. 'People will always try to pin you down and define you, but they'll always get it wrong. You're the only one who knows where you're really heading. And you're the only one who knows who you really are...'

Pitt was offered a host of parts, some of them to co-star with Juliette Lewis again. Jonathan Demme's follow-up to *Silence of the Lambs* was announced as being *Crazy for You*, a film about a mental patient who befriends an outcast in his ward. Pitt was up for the main role, which would have pre-figured his part in 1995's *Twelve Monkeys*. Pitt and Lewis were offered roles in Frank Military's courtroom murder mystery *Beyond a Reasonable Doubt*, which was turned down, as was a starring role for Pitt in *Baboon Heart*, later made as *Untamed Heart* (1993) with Christian Slater. Pitt also considered a role in *Devil's Advocate*, the tale of a hotshot lawyer entering a law firm, only to discover that it's run by the Devil. Al Pacino was talked about for the role of Satan and Joel Schumacher was down to direct, but the film didn't happen.

Whatever he did do next, to be taken seriously as an actor he would have to take risks to show his genuine, albeit developing, acting abilities. But, also, he could not afford another flop like *Cool World*.

At 55, Robert Redford was a mature Hollywood heart-throb who had gone through the experience that Brad Pitt was enduring. Cast initially for his pretty boy looks, Redford had triumphed over typecasting in front of the camera. He'd branched out from mere acting to writing and directing films, expressing his own political and environmental views in the process. He'd set up the Sundance Institute and Film Festival to promote new, young, independent film-making talent, and he already had a connection with Pitt, having played a hand in the script development of Tom DiCillo's *Johnny Suede*.

Having starred in the likes of *The Great Gatsby* (1974), *Butch Cassidy and the Sundance Kid* (1969, one of Brad Pitt's earliest film memories) and *All The President's Men* (1976), Redford's output had slowed down through the 80s, culminating in the big-budget flop *Havana* in 1990. He followed that with a starring role in *Sneakers* (1992), a high-tech computer thriller with an all-star cast that included Sidney Poitier, Dan Aykroyd and River Phoenix.

Redford's director's credentials were good, having won an Oscar for directing *Ordinary People* in 1980, but he had not been behind the camera since 1987's *The Milagro Beanfield War*. *A River Runs Through It*, Norman Maclean's autobiographical tale of a father and two sons who can only communicate through their shared passion for fly fishing, was close to Redford's heart, and he was determined to film it. 'This film is about a deeply loving family that did not understand each other. It's about how the ethic of pride affected them, and how to help someone you love before it's too late.'

Casting the roles was his greatest problem. He'd secured Craig Sheffer for the older MacLean brother, Norman, and had signed Tom Skerrit to play the father, but the role of Paul, the younger brother, a character who was both clever and doomed, was proving harder to fill.

One of the names that had come to mind for the part was that of River Phoenix, Redford's young co-star in *Sneakers*. Phoenix had enjoyed an unprecedented success as Hollywood's latest young pin-up during the late 80s. The young actor was ideal magazine feature material, with his bizarre south American childhood and unconventional upbringing by hippie parents. Phoenix had auditioned for Redford and was keen on the role, but doubtful that he would be cast. 'It's a great script,' he said. 'I auditioned – me and a thousand other guys. I had a good meeting with Redford, but I think he's gonna find the guy. The guy who is just that image – the Montana mountain boy, fly-fisherman image...' It turned out that 'the guy' was to be Brad Pitt.

Pitt was not yet such a big star that he could be cast in major roles without an audition. Unfortunately his first audition for the part of Paul Maclean had been, in his own word, 'shit'.

What looked to be the biggest and most challenging role of his career to date seemed to be slipping from his grasp. Determined to have another go, Pitt and his actor friend Dermot Mulroney – co-star with Bridget Fonda in *The Assassin* (1994) and later an investor/co-producer and star of Tom DiCillo's *Living in Oblivion* (1995) – got together with a video camera and taped a few scenes from the movie together. Pitt sent the tape off to Redford as a kind of unsolicited second audition. 'I think it kept me in there,' said Pitt of his unusual taped showreel.

Robert Redford had, in fact, been keeping close tabs on Pitt's growing reputation, especially because several commentators had already commented on the uncanny similarity in looks between him and Redford in his younger days. The older actor-director had discussed Pitt with *Cool World* director Ralph Bakshi, not once but three times, to determine whether he was worth hiring. Three times the answer came back, definitely yes! Having had his hopes independently confirmed, and having seen the tape, Redford was now prepared to cast him as the self-destructive younger brother.

Redford had no intention of featuring in the film himself, but one of the undoubted attractions of casting Brad Pitt was that the young actor could function as a surrogate for the director in the film, the way Woody Allen would later use John Cusack. Redford says he chose Pitt because he could embody the 'golden boy' aspects of Paul Maclean. 'There's no signs of trouble in his face,' said Redford, but Pitt also had the acting skills to capture the darker side of the character – the drinking and obsession with gambling that were to prove his downfall.

Fly fishing is both the main relaxation and a test of character for the Maclean family in *A River Runs Through It*, and Brad Pitt worked hard at mastering the techniques.

Robert Redford directs Brad and Craig Sheffer as two brothers in early 20th-century Montana in *A River Runs Through It*.

Four months before production began, Norman Maclean died. Redford had known the author for over five years, during which time he had struggled to convince him to release the cinema rights, sometimes in competition with other actors interested in the property, such as Oscar-winner William Hurt. Of Maclean's initial reluctance to have the film made, Redford said: 'I think he knew that in a small way he'd done something perfect. With it came all the pain and anguish of that time. Why risk all that by having it butchered on screen?' Following the author's death, Redford felt even more duty-bound than before to do the work justice.

Making the film presented a series of problems – many of which were inherent in the material. 'I thought this was a book that would be almost impossible to do,' admitted Redford. 'It has two elements – it is very literary and very lyrical. Film is not a literary medium, obviously, and in America at least, such things don't go down very well. Lyricism in film is treated with a great deal of cynicism. There were two hurdles right there.'

Shooting the film on location in Montana was important to Redford who was keen to capture, as much as possible, the feel for landscape from the original story. 'We couldn't use the original Big Blackfoot river, which is a very prominent river in the north west of Montana, near the town of Missoula, where the story took place,' lamented Redford. 'The idea was to film it on the actual river where Norman spent every summer of his life from childhood onwards. It was totally polluted from mining, the indiscriminate abuse of industry.'

It was impossible for a film that concentrated on fly-fishing for the principal actors to escape having to learn how to fish properly. Pitt threw himself into

Paul and Norman Maclean with their Protestant minister father
(Tom Skerrit, centre).

learning the craft – he wanted to look authentic on screen. After all, Paul was supposed to have a God-given gift for the sport, so he couldn't afford to look as if he didn't know how to fish for real. Opportunities to practise were few and far between, however, until he got to location. He'd try out his technique high atop Hollywood buildings. Occasionally he'd pop over to his friend singer Melissa Etheridge's house to use her swimming pool as a fly-fishing try out venue, a place to practise his casting technique in relative safety.

On location in Gallatin, 200 miles away from the Big Blackfoot River, Pitt was able to absorb the panoramic perfection of the landscape into his character – an important tip given to him by Redford. Pitt also got to play with antique collectors item fly-fishing rods – but only for close-ups. It was deemed too risky to have the neophyte fly-fisher let loose with the real 8ft Montague bamboo rods, originally used in the Montana of the 1820s.

Robert Redford enlisted the help of expert John Bailey to instruct his cast in the fine art of fly-fishing. While he came away from the film with more than a passing acquaintance with the sport, Brad Pitt got much more out of working with Robert Redford. He became aware that it was up to him to make sure other people knew what he was capable of. Redford offered advice, which Pitt took to heart. 'Hollywood is a business. It's very clear about what it is, very mercenary, and you have to work in that or around it. Once you understand that, you'll have a much better time.'

A River Runs Through It was welcomed by most critics, although many had reservations about its ability to draw a big audience given its limited-interest subject matter. However, most were pleased to see a film based on characters rather than slam-bam action.

In *The New Yorker*, Terrence Rafferty wrote of Pitt's character: 'Paul is mysteriously gifted at catching fish and mysteriously inept at living; the narrator tries, and fails, to connect the two mysteries.' *The Village Voice* played up the

Most of Pitt's scenes in *A River Runs Through It* are with his elder brother Norman
(Craig Sheffer), the narrator of the autobiographical story.

similarities between Pitt and Redford for all they were worth, suggesting that Redford's motives in casting Pitt were almost entirely narcissistic. 'A very clear line runs between Redford and Brad Pitt's golden boy,' wrote Georgina Brown. 'Wearing vintage suits, suspenders and fedoras, Pitt is a dead ringer for the young Redford of *The Sting* (1973). The camera dwells so lovingly on his toothpaste smile, manly jaw and sky blue eyes it seems that some narcissistic impulse is the true motive here.'

In Britain the reviews focused more on the film than the story's relatively obscure literary origins, and many hailed Pitt's performance as a significant breakthrough. *Empire* magazine, in particular, was full of praise. 'Pitt is a revelation, shedding his teen heart-throb image and turning in a layered performance that anchors the entire movie. It's a part Redford knows well and 20 years ago he would have played it himself.'

Others were as fulsome, with *The Independent*'s Adam Mars-Jones commenting 'Brad Pitt gives a particularly good performance'; *The Daily Telegraph* claimed that 'Brad Pitt is uncannily like a cross between James Dean and the young Robert Redford'; and Derek Malcolm in *The Guardian* thought 'it is well acted by Pitt in particular'.

'That was a beautifully crafted movie,' said Pitt of *A River Runs Through It*. 'Chiselled, you know. I'm not as satisfied with that performance as much, but the movie is so well done, it is bigger than any one performance.'

The press comparisons with the young Robert Redford seemed inevitable. 'It doesn't amount to much,' said Pitt of the constant references. 'Just what we need, hey, another sex symbol...Brad Pitt symbolises sex? I don't think so. They've never even been to bed with me...If that was all that I was known for when it's all said and done, I'd be disappointed. But hopefully I have more to offer than that...'

Although there was no sex in *A River Runs Through It*, Pitt was playing his by now standard clean-cut character, accentuating his good looks. If he was not entirely happy with his performance, perhaps it was because even Robert Redford was concentrating on how he looked and how he was lit, rather than on his acting and performance. Pitt didn't get to explore or display Paul's darker side as much as he would have liked – he had to wait to play Tristan in *Legends of the Fall* for that kind of part.

Although *A River Runs Through It* was certainly a step in the right direction for Pitt's career, at the end of it he found himself still confronting the same issues – how could he get the chance to surpass and escape his looks? Could he find a role that didn't depend on how he looked, but allowed him just to act, to show what he could do?

After Redford's film Brad Pitt made it clear to his agent that he was seeking something different, and his agent duly obliged, sending him a copy of a script entitled *Kalifornia*.

'I asked for it,' said Pitt of his decision to play the controversial role of serial killer Early Grayce. 'I picked the hardest one I could find. You take a movie because there's something it brings to you that you want to investigate. After *A River Runs Through It* I got this big label stuck on me and you want to remind the people that there's a little more going on than that. You can't go on doing the same thing over and over.'

This constant search for challenging material was to drive his career forward

A River Runs Through It is as much about growing up in a land still between wilderness and civilisation as it is about relationships.

from this point on, but Pitt hasn't looked at his career like his contemporary Johnny Depp. While Depp has pursued roles simply to please himself, almost deliberately carving out a quirky, box-office-avoiding career, Pitt has realised the importance of the business side of the film industry, something he'd learned from his old drama coach Roy London as well as from Robert Redford. He has known he has to alternate hit movies with films which might be more personally satisfying, but not such box office blockbusters. *Kalifornia* was his first step on that road.

The movie was to be a character piece, a showcase for four actors playing very different parts. The drama in this off-kilter road-movie-to-hell is kicked off by the character of Brian Kessler (played by David Duchovny, later to win international fame as Fox Mulder in the TV series *The X Files*). Kessler is a writer who is pleased – not to say self-satisfied – with his pet thesis on serial killers, which looks upon them as people to be pitied and helped, not condemned and jailed. His girlfriend Carrie Laughlin (Michelle Forbes, best known as the rambunctious Ensign Ro, one of Patrick Stewart's sparring partners in the TV series *Star Trek: The Next Generation*) is a photographer who takes sexually explicit pictures. Tired of their big-city life in New York and longing to move to California, the pair get the idea that they can combine their talents to produce an illustrated book on serial killers, the research giving them the opportunity to travel across the country. On the way they intend to stop off at infamous sites, the homes of serial killers or the venues of the

Kalifornia provided Brad Pitt with a different kind of part, that of Early Grayce, a serial killer with no redeeming features.

killings, take some pictures and notes for the text. The only problem is that they need to share the costs with two other passengers. Enter Early Grayce and Adele Corners, a real-life serial killer and his girlfriend who burst Brian's death-fantasy bubble by bringing a much-needed dose of down-and-dirty reality into his life.

Kalifornia was the feature film debut of director Dominic Sena whose previous film-making experience had been in the world of music videos. He'd directed clips for such acts as David Bowie, Sting, Elton John and Fleetwood Mac, as well as adverts for Estée Lauder perfumes, Coors, M&Ms, Lincoln Mercury and Chic Jeans. He started working with Tim Metcalfe's script in 1990, attracted by the main character. 'What caught my attention immediately,' said Sena of the screenplay, 'was the character of Early Grayce, this strangely likeable guy who just happens to be a serial killer.' Sena's producing partner Aris McGarry agreed: 'The most appealing characteristic of Early is his lack of consideration for the future, for the ramifications of his actions.'

Brad Pitt didn't see his as the leading part, though, feeling that all four characters were important to how the film was to work. '*Kalifornia* is like a musical quartet,' he said. 'Each character is integral to the whole as any other, and each must play in tune.'

Sena had to spend about 18 months working on the script, in between directing music videos, until he felt the characters were developed enough for him to decide to make the movie. 'While Early and Adele were pretty well drawn,' recalled Sena, 'we wanted to flesh out Brian and Carrie. Carrie needed more drive, so we made her a photographer gung ho on getting her boyfriend out to California. With him a writer and she a photographer, their collaboration on a book bonds the two and gives the stops during their road trip a purpose.'

Sena found his two leads for *Kalifornia* when viewing a videotape of *Too Young to Die?* the 1990 telefilm that had brought Pitt and Juliette Lewis together, professionally and personally. 'I was so excited when I saw her,' said Sena of Lewis. Part of his excitement came from the fleeting thought that he'd discovered a new talent. 'This was Adele – and better yet she's my discovery!' But he soon discovered that Martin Scorsese had beaten him to it by casting her in *Cape Fear*. Although fearing that she would now be outside the production's price range, Sena took a risk and sent her the script.

For some time Pitt and Lewis had been looking for another project to do together. Every time one or other was in a film the pair were separated for long periods of time – and the strain was beginning to show. Pitt had been in Montana for *A River Runs Through It*, while Lewis had been working with Scorsese and with Woody Allen on *Husbands and Wives*. Their careers were both well on track, but their personal lives were suffering. The way to deal with the problem was to work together on a film, just as they had done on *Too Young to Die?* It seemed that *Kalifornia* was the ideal opportunity, especially as the characters of Early and Adele were almost a reprise of the parts they'd played previously.

'Adele is like a ten-year-old girl,' thought Lewis of the character she was to play. 'She doesn't want to confront the severity of circumstances that surround her, so to maintain her innocence she sings songs, whistles, plays with her yo-yo, does anything to prevent her world from being overturned. She loves Early as someone who will be around her. He protects her.'

Sena had first seen Brad Pitt in *Thelma & Louise*, and coming across him in

Kalifornia gave Brad and Juliette Lewis the opportunity to work together again after three years of being forced apart by their different commitments for much of the time.

Too Young to Die? alongside Lewis gave him a ready-made serial killer couple. *Kalifornia* seemed to take as its starting point what might have happened to the characters of *Too Young to Die?* if they had not been caught at the film's climax.

Although his character was to be very different from anything else he had ever played, Pitt had two things to draw on. Firstly, although not as extreme, Billy Canton in *Too Young to Die?* had laid some of the basic groundwork for Early Grayce and, secondly, Pitt had known characters just like Early in his youth. 'Early Grayce is an animal,' Pitt said, simply. 'He's a little kid, a beer drinker. I've been familiar with guys like him. They kick cats around or stick firecrackers in their mouths. What drew me to this script was the questioning of why he does what he does.'

This character's look was very important, both to Pitt personally and to the production generally. Keen to escape his pretty boy image, Pitt was happy to get down and dirty for Early Grayce. He grew his hair long and added a scruffy beard. An accident also added to his appearance – he chipped one of his front teeth trying to crack open a bottle of Mountain Dew. Something most Hollywood stars would regard as a disaster and which would result in an emergency call to their orthodontist was actually welcomed. The 'defect' remained uncorrected until after the *Kalifornia* shoot was over and became part of Early Grayce's appearance.

Costume designer Kelle Kutsugeras, who had worked with Dominic Sena on

Brad Pitt grew his hair and a straggly beard for the part of Early Grayce, and had a tattoo and scars made up each day.

music videos for many years, had a clear view of the characters through their costumes: 'Early is dressed in trailer trash maximus,' joked Kutsugeras. 'His clothes come from whatever the workplace provided – mechanic pants and shirts. Adele wears polyester – it's built to last. Most of what she wears are 70s hand-me-downs, tube tops, floral dresses and wedgie cork shoes. Brian and Carrie, on the other hand, are very utilitarian – a lot of black, white and grey.'

Like Robert DeNiro in *Cape Fear*, Pitt also had to suffer some temporary body modification for the role. 'Brad didn't want his body to be clean,' recalled make-up artist Michelle Buhler, 'so he came up with this great tattoo idea for his forearm – a heart with the name that was once in it carved out.' Similar scars, wounds, burns and tattoo were placed on his body daily during production.

Production designer Michael White chose Atlanta as the location for the film because of its versatility. 'Atlanta has become an incredibly popular place to shoot lately, probably because it's a production designer's dream, with every type of location from worn-out urban decay to lush farmland.'

With the cross-country road trip taking the foursome of characters to some offbeat venues, White had a few challenges ahead. He avoided the usual method of hiring props from film studios, though, buying much of what was needed for the film's locations from thrift stores in the Atlanta area. 'Every place – Early's trailer, the diners, the motels, the mines, the abattoir – has either been forgotten or ignored. There's an uneasy, unsettling feeling about them.'

The five-week stay in Atlanta was taxing on the cast and crew. With much of the action taking place outdoors, weather became very important. High temperatures and higher humidity plagued the production, with record amounts of rain falling on the city during their stay.

Pitt viewed the film as 'something different...cops and robbers, and rubber guns and fake blood'. Taking childish delight in getting to play 'cops and robbers', Pitt got somewhat carried away. In his first big shooting scene, he had to blast away at a couple of policemen who are unlucky enough to stumble across the foursome. Take after take the sound man complained that there were weird noises on the tape. Eventually the problem was tracked down – every time he pulled the trigger on the prop gun he was using, Pitt was going 'Bam! Bam! Bam!'. 'I had no idea,' he said. 'I was like a little kid.'

Despite the 20 extra pounds he piled on, his long, lanky unwashed hair and scruffy beard, Pitt was still the centre of attention for many women on the set during production. Talking to *People* magazine, director Dominic Sena commented of Pitt: 'This guy just gets through to women, no matter what!'

The final four weeks of shooting on *Kalifornia* took place in the high deserts of California, where the temperatures reached 120 degrees F (49°C). While shooting in Barstow at 5am, a huge earthquake rocked the state, registering 7.4 on the Richter scale. The crew's location was only 40 miles from the epicentre, but no one was injured. Aftershocks, however, continued for weeks, unsettling many in the cast and crew as they wrapped production.

Having embarked on this risky role, Pitt found himself criticised by the movie press. Why didn't he stick to tried and tested roles? When was he going to play another JD? Did he take his clothes off in the new movie? Tired of the questioning, Pitt attempted to lay out what it was about the character of Early Grayce that had caught his attention, and he tried to explain why it was important personally to him

Early Grayce gets tough with Kessler (David Duchovny) in *Kalifornia*.

to play the part. 'Taking on a physically unappealing role was a help. Early was very far away from my own character and that was somehow easier.'

His choice to play such an unredeemed villain left many confused, just when they thought they'd got Pitt pigeon-holed. 'He doesn't have any redeeming features,' admitted Pitt of Early Grayce. 'But I like him. He's a killer but, you know, you can hear about someone who does something really horrible, then you begin to understand a little bit about where they came from. Some can overcome bad beginnings and become lawyers and doctor and have good families. Other people take great offence and shut off. This guy, Early Grayce, would have loved something in the beginning and been completely slammed down – where he gave up and had no feelings – so that killing someone meant no more than killing a bug. That's the way I saw him.'

There were some aspects to Early's character that audiences for *Kalifornia* didn't get to see, according to Pitt, either because they were cut from the film in favour of action material or were scripted but never shot in the first place. 'There was a scene that Early has with his father that I think we needed, even though it was the standard story of coming from a bad home. And in the original, there was more about his attraction to Carrie. We had such a low budget that we couldn't do it all.'

While pleased with the finished film, Pitt was not averse to seeing its problems. 'It's definitely a flawed movie,' he said, 'but it was a good time, too.' Release was limited, with its not coming out in Europe until two years after it had been shot, just like Pitt's earlier film *The Favor*. In America it came and went, making little impact on the box office. 'I went to bed one night and it was out, and I got up the next morning and it was gone!' Pitt joked. At least for Pitt big box office wasn't the point of *Kalifornia*. He'd had his chance to play against type and stretch his talents.

Many critics realised the unique look of the film and praised the lighting and direction, as well as the central performances. Despite those good points, though, most found the concept of the central character being a serial killer too discomforting to accept.

For Pitt the gamble had paid off, with American critics paying special attention to his against-the-grain performance. *The New York Times* noted: '*Kalifornia* confirms that Pitt is an interesting, persuasive actor,' while show business bible *Variety* felt moved to comment: 'the charismatic Pitt explores his character with quiet resolve, venting both horror and darkly comic implications'.

When belatedly released in Europe in 1994, *Kalifornia* received a mixed reception. Although seen as too pretentious for its own good, the film was recommended for its performances, particularly Pitt's. Typical was *Sight and Sound*. Criticising the film for its requirement that the viewer bring along a 'cultural studies primer', it nevertheless praised Pitt's performance: 'Not that Brad Pitt doesn't put in a show-stopping performance as Early Grayce, with an accent as thick as a mouthful of chewing tobacco and body language straight from *A Streetcar Named Desire* Brando. That is precisely one of the film's major problems – it is such an over-the-top performance that Early simply dominates the film and its other characters, making them little more than fellow passengers caught in his murderous tail-spin.'

Kalifornia was something Brad Pitt had to do. That the film was not a huge hit didn't matter – to those that were interested, particularly casting directors, *Kalifornia* was a calling card that presented a different side to Pitt's talents.

Work on *Kalifornia* was finished before *A River Runs Through It* hit cinemas, and confirmed Pitt as a rising Hollywood star. However, before the Hollywood machine totally took over Pitt had one more brief indulgence up his sleeve.

Following the success of *Reservoir Dogs* Quentin Tarantino found in 1993 that one of his screen plays that had been sold previously but not produced was being rushed into production. *True Romance* attracted a bunch of top stars to cameo roles because Tarantino was one of the few writers in modern Hollywood who provided speeches for actors to perform and dialogue they could get their teeth into. Hence people like Christopher Walken, Gary Oldman, Dennis Hopper and Val Kilmer all had small, but significant roles in the film.

Attracted to taking part in a project whose success or failure did not rest on his shoulders alone, Brad Pitt was quickly in contact with Tony Scott to see if there was a part in the movie he could play.

Christian Slater and Patricia Arquette were the leads, an unlikely on-the-run couple who have eloped with a suitcase full of stolen drugs which they aim to sell in Los Angeles and get rich on the cash. On arrival in LA, Slater's character Clarence

Brad's part as a dope-head in *True Romance* was only a cameo, but given the film's
high profile it greatly enhanced his reputation.

Worley looks up his best friend. Playing the best friend's permanently stoned
roommate named Floyd was Brad Pitt.

For the role Pitt spent his entire time lying about on a couch spouting variations
on surfer and valley speak, appearing at times to be involved in conversations
entirely different from those of the rest of the cast. It was a small, but showy role,
something most actors would positively jump at. As it was, Pitt – almost literally –
slept through the part. As various characters in the film came and went from the
house, Floyd's space oddity would offer them some drugs or the chance to watch a
bit of TV.

'That was fun,' reckoned Pitt of his brief star turn, 'but I was only there for a
few days.' Having read the script and told Tony Scott he liked it, the part was his,
no effort involved. Pitt particularly liked his role 'because he gets everyone killed'.
Pitt brought much to the character himself. 'I said, "Can I make him a stoner? A
pothead?" and he [Tony Scott] said, "Do whatever you want!"'

The laid-back atmosphere of the production, and the fact that the responsibility
of the film wasn't his, all added to Pitt's engagingly goofy performance. 'You know
Brad has a sense of mystery and a darkness, I think it comes from the chequered
life he had before,' Tony Scott said. 'That's a character that he knew and hung out
with at his house, this guy came for a week and stayed for two years – a pothead
who never got off the sofa.'

Pitt indeed had a real-life model to base the character on, a friend of his who'd
come to stay with him in Los Angeles for a short while, only to remain for many
months. Asked by *Empire* magazine if his friend had seen the film, Pitt answered:

'No, he's in an asylum, actually.'

Pitt's pothead friend may not have seen the movie, but many millions of others did. The combination of Tony Scott directing and Tarantino scripting, along with the all-star roster of cameos and Christian Slater as lead, was enough to ensure success. Even in his bit part, critics singled out Brad Pitt.

Variety highlighted the 'dopey fun in Brad Pitt's space cadet'. In among the cameos, *The Village Voice* commented that Brad Pitt 'almost steals home,' no mean feat up against well-known scene-stealers and scenery-chewers like Dennis Hopper, Christopher Walken and Gary Oldman. Writer Manohla Dargis noted a subtext in the film missed by many reviewers who chose instead to concentrate on the violence. 'If nothing else, the preponderance of pretty guys [Slater, Kilmer, Pitt] makes obvious that the film's real romance isn't between men and women, but men and men. Working the same homoerotic turf as *Reservoir Dogs*, Tarantino and Scott test the limits of fear, desire and masculinity with razor wit and surprising heart.'

In Britain it was the violence, rather than any sexual subtext, that grabbed the headlines, with many Conservatives clamouring for it to be banned following the withholding of *Reservoir Dogs*. Critics were no better disposed, calling it, variously, 'a bloody farce' in *The Independent on Sunday*, a 'pernicious' movie in *The New Statesman*, a movie that boasted a 'full compliment of fashionable violence' in *The Sunday Telegraph* and a 'noisy, vacuous fantasia' in *The Times*.

Some, however, did take a shine to the cameo performances, with Sheila Johnston in *The Independent* highlighting Pitt in 'a funny, unexpected role'. Hugo Davenport in *The Daily Telegraph* noted Pitt's 'perpetually stoned room-mate' and *The Guardian* mentioned 'Brad Pitt playing flat out (quite literally) as an LA space cadet, advanced grade'.

Whatever the reception of the role, Pitt wasn't in *True Romance* for the critical plaudits. Playing the part was a breeze and featuring alongside all those other actors in a prestigious and popular film like *True Romance* was not going to harm anyone's career. More importantly, his few days on the *True Romance* set, at the start of 1993, gave him the chance to come to a decision he had been putting off for sometime.

Kalifornia and *True Romance* were calling cards that Brad left with the industry to show that he could portray characters far removed from his normal image.

8 Playing Legends

HAVING wrapped up on *True Romance*, in February 1993 Pitt had finally decided to call off his long-lasting relationship with Juliette Lewis.

Pitt and Lewis had epitomised the then-fashionable grunge chic ethic, dressing down for film premieres and public appearances. But no matter how good (or bad) they looked together, Pitt and Lewis had spent much of their three years actually far apart from one another. Now Pitt was home from *True Romance*, Lewis was preparing to leave to shoot another Tarantino screenplay, Oliver Stone's *Natural Born Killers*.

They had, in fact, both been offered the lead roles, Mickey and Mallory, but Pitt hadn't been as interested in the material as Lewis. He had two reasons – he did not want to do another Early Grayce so soon after *Kalifornia*, and having just completed *True Romance* he was wary of doing another Tarantino script in quick succession.

During all the separations Pitt and Lewis had grown apart. Pitt was approaching 30, while Lewis was just still under 20. The age difference, which had not seemed so apparent before, was becoming an issue. There were other pressures - Lewis was keen to get married, and Pitt wasn't ready for such a serious commitment. 'She became very intense about their relationship,' a friend of the pair commented to *The National Enquirer* about their break-up. 'Brad became scared when Juliette started to tell friends that they would soon marry.'

Juliette was 'extraordinarily intense' according to another friend who spoke to *People* magazine about their split, 'but Brad is really the most laid-back young star I can think of.' Pitt had his own take on their doomed relationship: 'We were trying to be Sid and Nancy or something,' he said.

The pressures of work and the desire of one partner to get married and of the other to simply drift along, as he had done for most of his life, would be enough to strain any relationship to breaking point, especially one in the Hollywood spotlight. However, what was to drive the final wedge between them was Scientology.

The Church of Scientology had been found by 50s pulp science fiction author L. Ron Hubbard. The 'religion' claimed to be able to help people on the road to success, to be able to determine the negative emotions that hold someone back by 'auditing' them and then 'clearing' them. The courses involved in this process which the individuals have to undergo typically cost in the region of $300 to $400 per hour – a nice little earner for the Church and those that run it.

Healing the psychic scars caused by trauma in the present or in a past life is done with a device called an 'E-meter', invented by Hubbard. Students are then indoctrinated in the ways of the Church in a series of courses, with those who reach the higher levels learning of the secret mystery of Scientology. In something that sound like one of Hubbard's horrendous SF plots, according to the cult's theology (which only those in the upper hierarchy are supposed to know) an evil alien being called Xenu imprisoned other aliens under volcanoes on Earth 75 million years ago. The imprisoned aliens were then zapped by Xenu, leaving their spirits (or 'thetans')

Filming of *Legends of the Fall* produced strong differences of opinion between Brad Pitt and director Ed Zwick over the interpretation of Brad's role, Tristan.

93

to wander the Earth, attaching themselves to humans, thereby causing all sorts of psychic ills which could only be purged by Hubbard's patented 'technology'. Fiercely litigious, the cult has used the law and the courts to try and suppress its 'secret knowledge', a battle that continues in the 90s in cyberspace across the Internet.

It had been an aim of founder L. Ron Hubbard to recruit celebrities to his bogus operation as a way of spreading the message as early as 1955. According to John H. Richardson's exposé of Scientology activities in Hollywood in a 1993 issue of *Premiere* magazine, Hubbard had created something called Project Celebrity. A list of targets, including Orson Welles, Danny Kaye, James Stewart, Greta Garbo and Walt Disney, was drawn up and disciples were told to try and recruit them. Forty years later, after the establishment of the Celebrity Centre International on Franklin Avenue in LA, Hubbard had his wish.

The Hollywood honour role of recruits included John Travolta, Kirstie Alley and Tom Cruise. Cruise and his wife Mimi Rogers were both Scientologists, but his greater devotion to the cult was a factor in the break-up of their marriage (the prime one being their failure to have children). Other well-known names involved in the cult included Karen Black, Anne Archer, Kelly Preston and Nancy Cartwright, the voice of Bart Simpson on *The Simpsons*. When Michael Jackson's shock marriage to Lisa Marie Presley, Elvis Presley's daughter, was announced many thought it a Scientology plot to recruit Jackson, as she was an evangelical member.

Juliette Lewis had first become involved in the cult in the late 70s and early 80s through her father. She then became more active in the early 90s; for Pitt it was the last straw in their deteriorating relationship. 'Oh boy,' he exclaimed when the subject was raised by Britain's *Empire* magazine. 'Don't get me started! I'd go on for a couple of hours about that. The 30-second version is: I'm not big on anything that tells you how to live your life.'

Brought up by his Baptist parents to be tolerant of others, Pitt had tried humouring Lewis. He'd even attended some of the Scientology classes in Hollywood in an effort to get to the bottom of it, but he drifted into and out of the religion in short order. He was in good company. Others had taken this suck-it-and-see approach before quickly rejecting the creed, including Patrick Swayze, TV comedian Jerry Seinfeld and the late *Top Gun* producer Don Simpson, according to Richardson in *Premiere*.

Pitt's own struggle with his parents' religion had shown him the dangers of blind obedience, which seemed to be a key facet of Scientology's approach. It wasn't Lewis's involvement that Pitt disapproved of – it was just that he wanted to distance himself from anything that echoed his childhood religious experiences.

Since university Pitt had broken free from the people in his life who had tried to arrange his future for him – although they'd always done it with the best of intentions. In going unexpectedly to Hollywood, he had struck out in a direction that was truly his own, not dictated by his parents or by the expectations of his local community or peers. More importantly, he'd succeeded. He wasn't about to step backwards into a lifestyle where rules and regulations would govern his life once more. He was too independently minded for that.

Keeping it in the family is common in Scientology – Travolta married fellow cult member Kelly Preston; Cruise's second wife, Nicole Kidman, was also a member; while actor brothers Charlie Sheen and Emilo Estevez had been the target of recruitment attempts through their girlfriends (the same Kelly Preston in Sheen's case). But despite their relationship, Lewis did not try to recruit Pitt into the cult. 'I wasn't under any pressure at all,' he said. 'You've got to see what's going on if your love's into it, because you've got to respect your love.'

Pitt was happy for Lewis to go her own way, and if that meant getting more involved with Scientology, so be it. By his own ethics and standards, he felt he couldn't interfere, although he didn't approve. He said: 'Whatever helps you sleep at night, whatever helps you get up in the morning. As much as I don't want anyone telling me how to live my life, I can't tell someone how to live theirs.' For Pitt, Scientology was not his thing. 'It's bad for me,' he admitted, 'but I know it made my girl feel better.'

Their three years together now over, Pitt and Lewis vowed to remain friends and possibly even work together again in the future. 'I'd work with her again in a second. You could have some powerful stuff out there. I still love the woman. There's some real genius there. I had a great time with her,' Pitt told *Vanity Fair*. 'She has her own views. It was one of the greatest relationships I've ever been in. The problem is, we grow up with this vision that love conquers all, and that's just not so, is it?'

It took a long time for Lewis to get over the break-up, and even in 1995 talking with Quentin Tarantino in *Details* magazine she still felt strongly about the end of their affair. 'From 16 to 20, I was with one person and truly, truly in love,' she said, 'and then all these elements in his life and mine were changing, and those are enormous years as it is...'

One of the major problems for her was that the pair didn't so much break-up as continue to drift apart until they simply stopped being together. Their relationship lacked a final dramatic closure. 'It wasn't cut and dried, it wasn't totally breaking up, so I lost myself there for a second,' Lewis said. 'I felt bad about myself, and the thing about doing movies when you're going through personal stuff is that you've got to feel good enough to be in front of a camera. It's a distant thing now, but a couple of years ago it was a huge change, and I had to remember that I had once lived alone, and had my own pride and my own ideas. There was much more to it than the relationship, it was also where I was in my life. It's old now, and I actually care about Brad and I think he and Gwyneth are cool. I think he's found a good girl.'

Following his break up with Lewis, Pitt moved out of their shared home, packing all his stuff into the back of a car, including his antiques, his huge and disorganised CD collection, his cherished espresso machine and his equally cherished guitars.

Moving into a temporary rented apartment, Pitt couldn't seem to settle down. He wasn't used to living alone - for years he'd either been on film sets or at home with Lewis. There'd always been company around. Out of work and out of Lewis's life, he was at a loose end and he found it difficult to occupy himself. Never a big reader, he'd while away the evenings watching indifferent movies on TV, or else he would find himself heading out into LA in the evenings, driving around and stopping off in bars. He was candid about that period: 'The main reason I used to go to bars was to pick up girls.'

During 1993 Pitt was offered a variety of roles which he turned down, in addition to the lead in *Natural Born Killers*. He also turned down an approach from his *Thelma & Louise* director Ridley Scott to take part in his proposed film

Pancho's War to play a 1916 Mexican revolutionary who is a munitions expert delivering guns to General Pershing. The film was scrapped as it was in competition with another similar film, *Tom Mix & Pancho Villa*, to be directed by Scott's brother Tony. Eventually neither film was made.

Producer Edward Zwick easily recalled Brad Pitt's impact during his one guest shot appearance on the TV show he was producing. Pitt's brief monosyllabic turn in *thirtysomething* had not only been noticed by audiences, but the young actor's early performance had stayed in Zwick's memory.

An Emmy-award winning TV writer, producer and director, Ed Zwick had ambitions in the cinema. He began his feature film career with *About Last Night...* (1986), a teen movie adaptation of David Mamet's play *Sexual Perversity in Chicago*. He followed that with *Leaving Normal* (1992), a sort of imitation *Thelma & Louise*, featuring Meg Tilly and Christine Lahti. Zwick's own strong interest in American history led to *Glory* (1989), a Civil War epic starring Matthew Broderick and Denzel Washington, who secured the Best Supporting Actor Oscar for his performance.

Since reading Jim Harrison's novella *Legends of the Fall* in a 1978 edition of *Esquire* when he was 26 and studying at LA's American Film Institute, Zwick had harboured ambitions of one day making it into a movie. 'Reading it was a very moving experience,' recalled Zwick. 'It has held its power over me all these years of trying to turn it into a film. It's a big, dark, beautiful and generous family chronicle. At once a great story, and also a kind of meditation on the humility and dignity of man.'

'I called the agents and publishers,' said Zwick of the beginning of his 17-year fight to bring the story to the screen, 'but I was still in film school and they laughed at me and told me the rights were owned by other people.'

Harrison's short novel tells an epic tale – that of the Ludlow family in the early years of the 20th century. The father and three brothers live an isolated existence on a ranch in the foothills of the Rocky Mountains. Col. William Ludlow had retreated there after he left the US Cavalry in protest at the authorities' treatment of the Western tribes of American Indians. Separated from his ambitious, city-living wife, Ludlow tries to raise his three sons in the country away from the madness of the times.

Alfred is the eldest brother, and the most dutiful and reserved, while Samuel is the impetuous, idealistic youngest of the trio. In between comes Tristan, a wild, untamed spirit, full of animal passion and wise in the ways of the Indians, having come under the tutelage of his father's old Cree Indian scout, One Stab.

The three brothers were inseparable growing up, but with maturity come challenges, both personal and professional, and the trio do not know what trials the modern world they are unprepared for will throw at them. Beginning with the outbreak of the First World War, the story follows the lives of the three and their involvements with one woman, Susannah. Epic in scale, but personal in nature, *Legends of the Fall* was ideal material for Zwick to follow *Glory*.

The main challenge for Zwick was casting the central role of the middle brother, Tristan. It was one he answered easily, as Brad Pitt leapt immediately into his mind. Since he'd had experience of working with Pitt early on in his career, Zwick had followed the actor's developing Hollywood persona, and was convinced he was right

'Brad had a very strong, intuitive understanding of his character.' (Edward Zwick)

for the role.

Zwick had sent Pitt an earlier draft of the script two years before the film was ready for production, hooking the actor's interest in the project. 'He'd not even done *Thelma & Louise* then. Not many people know that he'd done two days' work on *thirtysomething* and we started to meet and talk about this role while his career began to unfold.'

Pitt committed in principal to playing the part when Zwick finally got the project off the ground. The family saga had struck a chord with him too. 'A lot of the elements are very strange,' felt Pitt of the *Legends of the Fall* story, 'western, war, love triangle, family, killings – right? It's bold, it's big, like a great bottle of wine or something.'

'He was quite passionate about it,' said Zwick of Pitt's interest. Zwick was intending to defer his salary until after the film started earning from box office receipts in order to get it made, and he managed to persuade Pitt also to defer part of his $3 million salary, even though as his career sky rocketed, so did his asking price. 'One way we got this movie made was for me to defer a significant part of my salary and for Brad to become my partner, doing that for himself as well. As I struggled to get the movie made, I was able to see his work as it began to emerge. It's a very difficult thing to embody the kind of lifeforce that this character has and you had to be willing to take certain emotional risks and certain challenges. I knew the toughest role belonged to Tristan, but how do you send out a casting call for a force of nature? It became obvious Brad was the right choice, but the studio was hesitant, and it wasn't until I got Anthony Hopkins [as the father, Col. Ludlow] that they gave us the go-ahead. I think, frankly, it was Brad's involvement that encouraged them, and Tony's that cemented it.'

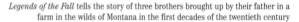

Legends of the Fall tells the story of three brothers brought up by their father in a farm in the wilds of Montana in the first decades of the twentieth century

Tristan, the middle in age of the three brothers and the one played by Brad, is the pivotal character of the film. The others are played by Aidan Quinn (left) and Henry Thomas (second right) with Anthony Hopkins (second left) as their father

'I've always thought that there would be someone better for most of the roles I've taken,' said Pitt candidly. 'But I knew I was the best one to play Tristan. I knew it the minute I read it. I knew the corners, I knew the bends in the road, knew exactly where it went. My difficulty was in trying to get others to see it the way I did. Films are very exhausting to make, so you'd better pick something that means something to you, and this one did.'

For Zwick, Pitt and Tristan had much in common. 'Brad had a very strong, intuitive understanding of his character. I think there is a great deal of Tristan within him. I know he has challenged himself to explore some of the darker aspects of his character as well as the more romantic qualities.' Yet, their instinctive feeling for the material and their admiration for each other were not to prevent Pitt and Zwick later disagreeing over exactly how the emotions of the story should be filmed.

During his long struggle to get the film underway, much had happened in Zwick's life. He had married, had children, enjoyed professional success and failure and lived through his brother's death. It all fed his determination to make this family saga his way. 'I relate to a man's life being defined by his losses and grief as well as his victories. Tristan is a wish-fulfilment for all of us, someone who expresses the most primitive of thoughts we all have, and acts on them, unbound by convention.'

Once production on the tightly budgeted $32 million project was underway, filling the other leading roles was easy work. One of Zwick's coups was to audition a young actor named Henry Thomas, who had sprung to fame as Elliot in Steven Spielberg's magical *E.T.–The Extraterrestrial* (1982), the little boy who befriends an alien stranded on Earth. 'I was auditioned for the role before anyone was cast beside Brad,' recalled Thomas. 'Then I heard Aidan Quinn was in it, and I thought "Oh, it's getting better and better.' Then I heard Anthony Hopkins, and I was like, "Oh wow, I hope I get this." And then finally, after they cast Julia [Ormond], they cast me, and a week later rehearsals started.'

With Thomas as younger brother Samuel, rising British actress Julia Ormond as his fiancée Susannah, and Aidan Quinn as eldest brother Alfred alongside Hopkins and Pitt, *Legends of the Fall* was ready to roll. Pitt and Zwick had flown to London on a red-eye flight to tape a hurriedly arranged screen test with Ormond, who had become a hot property on the back of a stage performance of *Wuthering Heights*. After *Legends of the Fall* she went on to star as Guinevere opposite Sean Connery as King Arthur in *First Knight* (1995) and opposite Harrison Ford in the title role of *Sabrina* (1995).

After the casting, the next hurdle awaiting Zwick and his team was finding the right location to shoot the film. Some scenes were filmed on location in Vancouver, British Columbia, but the majority were shot on the Stoney Indian Reserve outside Calgary, Alberta. One of the reasons for shooting in southern central Canada – apart from saving the production $2 million due to an advantageous exchange rate – was the weather. The area is traditionally one of the driest parts of the country. However, the weather decided to break with tradition as the *Legends* crew arrived to begin filming. It turned out to be fortuitous. 'Of course, the movie wouldn't be as beautiful if we didn't have that extraordinary weather,' recalled Zwick. 'Everything you see in the movie is before a storm hit or just after one hit – but it certainly made things tough. For every beautiful cumulus cloud you see, you don't see three hours of us huddling under these awful tarps with lightning striking the dolly.'

So it was that in the summer of 1993 Brad Pitt found himself spending a gruelling, rainy three months in Calgary, throwing himself heart, body and soul into the role of Tristan. He rented a cabin in the foothills of the Rockies and every Saturday night, as an antidote to the stresses of playing his character and to the tensions beginning to develop between him and Zwick, bouts of silliness would break out. 'We re-created the *Blazing Saddles* scene around the bonfire a few times,' laughed Pitt. 'I must say, Aidan Quinn, he's quite impressive. A lovely little Indian girl who worked on the movie, named Sekwan, dubbed Aidan "Wind in his Pants". Then we dubbed her "One Who Sniffs the Wind".'

Rumours flowed from the location filming to tabloid newspapers that Pitt – who was, after all, well-known for romancing his leading ladies – and Ormond were more than mere co-stars. Both denied that sharing the rented cabin during production indicated any deeper relationship.

Legends of the Fall was intended to be a blockbuster from the beginning and Brad Pitt had a huge task ahead of him. Although sharing the spotlight with the two other brothers and with Oscar-winner Anthony Hopkins, it was Pitt who was to carry the film. His character is the centre of the drama. His actions – or lack of them – affect the lives of all around him. Although he was not present in every scene, Tristan's spirit suffuses the film, and it was important that when he was on screen that he had an impact. For Pitt, this performance would require all of his skills and all of his experience. He would draw on every role he'd played to date, combining the squeaky clean good looks of Paul in *A River Runs Through It* with the darker aspects of characters like Early Grayce or Billy in *Too Young to Die?*.

It may have been the pressure of the performance, or simply the fact that Zwick

Several scenes of *Legends of the Fall* were shot in Jamaica, covering for New Guinea, Africa and the South Seas.

had committed many years of his life to the project, but early on it was clear there was going to be a major difference of opinion between the director and the star over the interpretation of Tristan. When he realised he had a conflict with Pitt, Zwick couldn't simply recast the role as he might have done with any other hired actor. He'd interested the studio on the back of Pitt's name, the star was his partner in the production, he was genuinely friendly with Pitt and he needed his presence to pull in the mass audience he hoped for. He had no choice but to manage what was to become a difficult situation.

Filming during the first week of shooting included a scene important to the climax of the film in which Susannah visits Tristan behind bars. There was another reason too: Pitt had already committed to another movie, *Interview with the Vampire*, and to be ready to start on time his scenes in *Legends* had to be shot early in the production. It was too early for Pitt, however, who didn't feel the scene was ready to be committed to film. 'The jail scene wasn't right, wasn't written right, didn't fit in,' he said. 'When we shot it I said, "This is a mistake."'

Zwick, however, mindful of his tight schedule, was loath to get behind and miss this opportunity to clear what he felt was an easy scene to shoot. He believed that Pitt hadn't reached the right point emotionally to play the scene, not that it was badly written. 'You have to be quite careful finding your stepping-stones, because it's all out of order,' said Zwick, sympathising with his star's quandary.

According to *Premiere*, though, this encounter turned violent, prompting the crew to clear the set. Furniture was said to have flown through the air. 'If a chair or a stool was thrown,' said an on-set source, 'it certainly wasn't thrown at anybody...' The scene was filmed, but Zwick told co-producer Marshall Herskovitz (his partner from *thirtysomething*) that he would have to find time later in the shoot to film the scene again, as neither director nor actor were happy with it as it currently stood.

'Brad had to internalise an enormous amount to express a scene's truthfulness,' said Zwick. 'The explorations he's asked to make in this part are difficult. Sometimes when I'm directing, I feel like an interpreter at the United Nations. Sure, we went at it, and that too is part of the process. Certainly by the next morning we were contrite and desperately eager to make up, not hold onto it, and go on to the next thing.'

Pitt was equally diplomatic after the incident. 'Yeah, Ed and I had a tough day that day, which is good. It's good if two people care. Have at it, 'cause at the end you're going to come up with something good – and that was the result in the jail scene we got now. This time it was written right, it was done right.'

Although that particular dispute was resolved, it was not a good start to the production. There was a widespread fear among the crew that tension between star and director would rear its ugly head once again and might even continue on through the coming weeks of heavy production.

The Hollywood rumour mill went into overdrive as the first stories of on-set disputes filtered back to the LA film community. 'There was all this press that came out that we were not getting along, these rumours in Hollywood that it's not going right,' said Pitt of the early production period in Calgary. 'You know, this is a gamble, and even TriStar's gambling on me, putting me in this kind of movie. So people want to hear it's going bad. I find myself having to defend Ed, 'cause these rumours are going around. But that hasn't been the case; it's been pretty easy-going.'

Pitt seemed to get on better with the other members of the cast than he did with his director. He worked particularly closely with Julia Ormond, the woman around whom the lives of the three brothers revolve, and with whom he was sharing the rented cabin. 'We've had a lot of dying and crying on this one,' said Pitt. 'Julia has this kind of timeless class that I haven't seen anywhere else. The shooting was in a remote spot. At night, the guys all just sat around a campfire and Henry [Thomas] played his guitar. Julia brought a whole library of books. She read, and wrote, all the time. She wrote a diary of the filming.'

Pitt had pushed Zwick to cast Aidan Quinn, whose work he had admired, in the role of his older, more down-to-earth brother. 'It's probably the toughest part in the movie,' felt Pitt. 'It could easily have gone wimpy. We needed somebody who'd be equal to Tristan, bringing nobility and strength to the role, and sexiness, of all things, and that's Aidan.'

For his part, Quinn saw a maturing of Brad Pitt during filming. 'I happened onto some dailies that were on tape, and saw him at that grave, and he was just devastating.

Julia Ormond was rumoured to have had an off-screen relationship with Brad, as well as an on-screen one.

Brad's got a very traditional, manly kind of persona, so to see that man fighting the emotion and not winning – there was stuff he was adding that wasn't even scripted – was just so powerful, watching it spill out.'

Thankful to his co-star for getting him the part, Quinn was not above making light of the areas where Pitt, quite literally, fell down. 'I'm not a horseman, but I never fell off my horse, like some people who shall remain nameless,' he said of Pitt. 'He actually called the studio to get me hired. They wanted a bigger name, but he wanted me.'

Inevitably, *Legends of the Fall* provided another love scene for Pitt – this time with Julia Ormond. Conditions on the set were, however, not at all conducive to the action. 'It's not the most romantic setting, y'know,' said Pitt of shooting on a plywood set in the middle of a Calgary curling rink. 'Very anti-erection...'

To get in the mood, director Zwick allowed Pitt to play his choice of music on the set – hence he and Ormond attempted to convince the movie-going public of their passion for one another while Toad the Wet Sprocket's 'Fear' played on a nearby ghetto blaster. 'You throw a little music on and you try to forget about all the people staring at you,' said Pitt of his approach to love scenes. It was a technique he'd been using successfully since playing JD. 'I got that, actually, from Ridley [Scott], because he let us play music during that Geena Davis scene.'

In fact, using music is central to the method in Brad Pitt's acting. Far from hailing from the Method Acting school, epitomised by Marlon Brando and James Dean, Pitt claims to be intuitive in his skills and talent. 'I don't know much about acting. I don't know what the hell I'm doin'. I just don't.'

One thing he does know, though, is how to use music to get him into the mood of the character he's playing. 'That's what works best for me,' he claimed, citing Stevie Ray Vaughan as inspiration on *Legends of the Fall*. (Pitt was to consider playing Vaughan in a proposed biopic in 1996.) For his next film, *Interview With the Vampire*, Pitt would get into character by playing bits of Mazzy Star and The Doors, as well as some Blind Melons and Smashing Pumpkins. Early Grayce in *Kalifornia* was a different matter: 'That was more heavy metal...'

Pitt strives to avoid assuming any kind of identification with his characters – he doesn't want to absorb or take home from the set any of the characteristics of the people he plays, a problem many Method actors suffer. 'Somewhere in the third or fourth week, you respond to things a little differently, like your character would respond. I don't like it,' he told *Vanity Fair*. 'I can't wait to get my own clothes back on, listen to some good music, eat what I want to eat. Movies are very complicated. You don't realise what it takes to get a good movie. Sitting home in Missouri, I sure didn't. It's fun for a little while. Then I'm ready to get back into my own boxers...' However, avoiding being taken over by a character was not always to be easy, and was to become a problem in *Legends* and even more so during the production of *Interview With the Vampire*.

Despite the jibes of Aidan Quinn, horse riding was a key skill required in *Legends of the Fall*. It was something Pitt had never done before, but he was required on screen to look like someone who'd ridden horses all his life. He threw himself into learning how to deal with horses properly, refusing to cheat through editing and swift cutting or by using a double. If the script called for Tristan to mount a horse, Brad Pitt was going to learn how to do it convincingly. 'Listen, you just grab the pommel and kick,' he said.

His new found easiness with horses came in handy during the shoot when the young actor playing his son took fright at having to ride one of the beasts. Pitt sat down with him and told him: 'Look, we took this job, we have to do this scene, but you don't have to do anything you don't want to do. If you don't want to ride on the horse, you can ride in the car. But I'm going to ride on the horse, because I like the horse.'

Pitt's approach was in marked contrast to that of other members of the crew, and was enough to convince the young actor onto the animal. According to Pitt: 'What they were doing to him when I walked up was going, "But don't you want to ride on the horse. It's a magic horse! Na-na-na-na-na." Talking to him like a moron, y'know. That's when we went for our little walk and I told him, "You don't have to do anything you don't want to do." It's that simple. You can always find a way to make something feel right.' Pitt had clearly absorbed some lessons from his own father's thoughtful treatment of him while younger.

The epic sprawl of *Legends of the Fall*, both in geography and through history, had to be captured on a very tight budget. 'I used all my experience in TV of how to stretch your dollars a long way – that's something I take pride in... My background is in theatre, where suggestion is important. We had 800 people one night during a war scene, but then only 300 the next night and then the other two nights we had 100 people. Yet the size seemed much larger because we kept the frame alive.'

Zwick also stretched his budget-busting skills to their maximum extent to film scenes in which Tristan tries to escape his grief and responsibilities by adopting the life of a sailor. 'We went to Jamaica for three days and in that time we made Jamaica be New Guinea, Africa, and the South Seas in a boat. We did all this with little things created only in one direction for the lens to see and you and your imagination to fill out,' said Zwick. However, his less-is-more philosophy led to some of these scenes not making the final cut. 'There is almost a way in which this movie was deliberately illustrated like a book, with one strong image rather than a five-minute sequence.'

At the end of his taxing time in Calgary, and after the battles with Zwick over the direction of his character and the role he would play in the film, Pitt was satisfied with his work – and up to this point, he had been his own harshest critic. 'This has been a good deal,' he told *Premiere* as the shoot wrapped. 'It's been the hardest thing I have tried to tackle, and as I look back, finishing up, it's been good – to work hard.'

Pitt's opinion changed somewhat when he saw the final cut. The tensions that had been exhibited during the shooting of the jail scene and that had rumbled on during production came to a head. The film he watched was not the one that he felt he'd made. 'Our process was not without tensions, passions,' said Zwick of Pitt's problems with the finished film. 'Brad has great artistic impulses, great instincts. But in the acting world, he skipped a lot of steps. He's no less emotional, but he's less obviously expressive, and the role required real self-revealment. Where he's from you keep that stuff to yourself...'

Pitt objected to the scenes featuring his character's descent into madness being cut from the film. The actor felt that they were necessary to show the process by which Tristan eventually reaches redemption. Zwick claimed the scenes were cut to give space to the other characters in the film. That wasn't how Pitt saw things, though. 'By taking out so much as they did, the movie becomes too mushy, 'cause there's no space in between the mush,' claimed Pitt. 'If I'd known where it was going to end up, I would have really fought against the cheese. There are moments where, if it was reduced to that, if that's all we were going to see of him, I would have whittled it down. I wouldn't have shown so much.'

Zwick simply accepted Pitt's intense nature and need to contribute to the development of his character. 'Of course he's intense,' said the director. However, he felt equally strongly that it is the director's right to call the shots, to decide what gets used and what doesn't and how, exactly, the characters should develop and how he should get the performance he wants from his actors. 'As a director you learn to communicate with the individual actor according to his individual needs – and God knows, Brad and I spent a lot of time getting to know each other, trying to understand each other's process.'

Pitt was more open about his side of the dispute: 'People want to hear that we were not getting along. You read things in scripts and envision them. I didn't want

my character to show his cards so blatantly and Ed did. So you've got two people who care about the film and the character and we had different views. Fortunately, something good is going to be squeezed out of that...'

Generally, critics agreed with Pitt that *Legends of the Fall* - after the struggle between star and director over the films direction - turned out to be better than merely 'good'.

It was released in December 1994, a month after *Interview With the Vampire*, which he filmed immediately afterwards. The critics either loved it or hated it. Ben Greenman in *The Village Voice* was definitely in the former camp: 'The real focus of the film is Pitt's Tristan. Deeply divided – lover and loner, brutal warrior and spiritual introvert – Tristan toes the line between rugged hero and a man whose appetite for solitude borders on the pathological. While Pitt was anaemic in *Interview*, he proves here that he can inhabit a character without sacrificing his own charisma. With the physicality of the young Brando, he dominates not only the screen but the audience, and even the clutter and cliché of the film's final hour cannot dim the power of his performance...'

People magazine tried to hedge its bets: 'It either sweeps you up in its rapturous wake or ... you just sit there and snicker.' Others concentrated on Pitt's performance. 'Star making,' said TV critics Siskel and Ebert, while *Rolling Stone* announced: 'Pitt carries the picture. The blue-eyed boy proves himself a movie star stealing every scene he's in.'

Released in Britain in April 1995, the film was received in similar fashion. *Sight and Sound* critic Ben Thompson got quite caught up in the overblown spirit of the movie: 'An epic performance from Brad Pitt. The first time we see him riding across the plains as a full grown adult, his brother tells him, "You smell". He doesn't just smell, he positively reeks – his machismo all but fogs up the screen...Brad Pitt is a god on horseback. He ropes steers, he steers ropes, he prowls the high country in a selection of beautifully starched fabrics. And when things go wrong for him emotionally, he does what all men long to do: he grows his hair long, and goes out into the world to kill things...'

As far as British critics were concerned, Brad Pitt was the main reason for going to see *Legends*. *The Daily Mail* didn't mince its words: 'Brad Pitt is Hollywood's fastest-rising sex symbol and here he chooses to follow in the footsteps of James Dean, with a sprawling family saga which is even bigger than *Giant*.' Even *The Financial Times* got caught up in Pitt-mania: 'Brad Pitt is eminently watchable as he portrays this youthful energy smashing against the rocks of a tumultuous world ... his performance is shot through with a barely controlled passion...'

Legends of the Fall was the first major film where Pitt was to be the main draw. His casting had to, in Hollywood parlance, 'open' the film - attract a big enough audience in the first few weeks of release to ensure that the picture was deemed successful, at least economically, if not also artistically.

The period between *True Romance* and *Legends of the Fall* had been a difficult one for Pitt, after the break-up of his long relationship with Juliette Lewis. Although he initiated it, the split had thrown him into a depression from which his work had rescued him. More work was just what he needed, and before embarking on *Legends of the Fall*, he had made the commitment to the film version of Anne Rice's *Interview With the Vampire*. Before donning the fangs, though, Brad Pitt had to make room for a new woman in his life...

Brad had little time to relax between the end of the shooting of
Legends and the start of *Interview with the Vampire*.

9 The Reluctant Vampire

BRAD PITT's solitary existence after his split from Juliette Lewis had come to an end during his days of cruising Los Angeles bars. Attending a party he'd struck up a friendship with a 24-year-old actress named Jitka Pohlodek, who claimed to be from Czechoslovakia 'by way of Arkansas'. Hitting it off – Pitt nicknamed his new girlfriend Yit – the pair were soon living together in Pitt's newly bought home.

Having taken his time to find just the right property after splitting with Juliette Lewis, Pitt had settled on a 1910 Craftsman house high in the Hollywood hills. It featured terraces and balconies all around, with a pool and a pond, as well as a man-made cave which Pitt kitted out with an Oriental rug, and also boasted a rooftop recreation area which Pitt kitted out as an alfresco bachelor pad, featuring a sofa, a coffee table and a CD player. 'It gets rained on,' said Pitt of his high up hideaway.

Music being central to Pitt's way of working, it is also key to his relaxation. His haphazardly arranged collection of CDs was spread throughout the house, and choosing music tended to be a random lucky dip. 'It's kind of ... you're on the search. You just find the right one for the needed moment.' Except when Yit moved in with him, Pitt got organised and attempted to catch up on some Rolling Stones stuff. 'This woman that I'm kinda hanging out with, she thinks Mick is it!'

Pitt and Yit were never going to be a long-term deal, and it seems both knew it when they moved in together. Working on both *Legends of the Fall* and *Interview With the Vampire* back to back didn't allow Pitt much time to spend with her.

When she moved in, though, Yit brought a new addition to Pitt's menagerie of animals. Her two bobcats joined his three dogs, all anointed with unusual names. 'This one is Todd Potter, this one is Saudi - she's a pound dog, she loves the love – and this one is Purty, 'cause he's so damned purty,' he explained to *Vanity Fair*. 'I buy my dogs chocolate treats, chew bones, all that kind of stuff. I love it when they can smell what it is and they rip all the wrapping paper off.'

The newest additions to the Pitt animal menagerie brought associated problems. 'Believe me, one of our biggest concerns is keeping the bobcats completely free. Not caged in like a bird, which blows my mind, cutting its wings,' said Pitt. 'I do not understand that. Cutting a dog's tail off for the way it looks. In fact I'm going to start a cause, Save the Tails. All us young actors, we have causes, that's going to be my cause, Save the Tails.'

Inside his new home, Pitt installed copper walls embossed with leaves and the furniture consisted of big old wood-and-leather sofas and chairs, some guitars for jamming on and built-in glass cabinets, crammed with CDs. Out in the back area of the building, he did have some animals in cages – 40 chameleons, kept in Chinese-lantern-shaped boxes.

For his next film, straight from wrapping *Legends of the Fall*, Brad Pitt brought his own chameleon-like attributes to the fore. He was to play a reluctant vampire in the movie version of a book that enjoyed a loyal and vocal following.

The story of the film version of Anne Rice's novel *Interview With the Vampire* is

'I saw everything he'd done and he is just absolutely captivating.' (Neil Jordan).

109

a lengthy and tortuous one. Rice, who also writes soft-core pornographic fiction, wrote the first of her vampire novels in 1976, shortly after her five-year-old-daughter, Michele, died tragically of leukaemia. In reaction to this personal tragedy she set about exorcising her demons and her anger with the world by creating a cast of vampire characters. She dreamed up a lost soul in the character of Louis De Ponte Du Lac, a 19th-century plantation owner in New Orleans, who, in despair after the death of his family, succumbs to the seduction of the charismatic Lestat de Lioncourt. A vampire, Lestat offers Louis a release from his earthly suffering by turning him into a blood-sucking creature of the night.

Even that is not enough to relieve Louis's suffering, and he begins to tire of merely being Lestat's creation. Lestat responds by turning a small girl, Claudia, into a third vampire to function as his companion.

Publishers steered clear of the novel, finding it too dark and disturbing to publish, until the prestigious Knopf Books decided to take the risk. The book struck a chord and went on to become a best-seller, spawning a series of sequels which attracted a cult following.

Naturally on the back of a successful book came talk of making it into a film, but it took over 18 years to go from option to production. The movie rights were, in fact, optioned for $150,000 even before the book went to press.

The hottest Hollywood actor of 1976, John Travolta, was pencilled in for the part of Lestat. However, it wasn't a good time to be considering a new vampire movie as the market was already saturated: Frank Langella was playing the title part in *Dracula*, while George Hamilton played the same role for laughs in *Love at First Bite*. In the face of this competition, Paramount decided to hang fire on *Interview With the Vampire*, anticipating a second novel they could incorporate into the script. This book, *The Vampire Lestat*, however, didn't appear until 1985, almost a decade later.

In the sequel Lestat had become a rock star. Paramount was unhappy with this and dropped its option. The right to both books passed to Lorimar Television, who planned to produce them as a TV mini-series starring Richard Chamberlain. That version didn't get off the ground either, and other formats were considered, including a musical by Elton John to star Sting and Cher in the lead roles.

By January 1989 Warner Brothers had purchased Lorimar, and with the company came the rights to the Anne Rice books. Producer and record mogul David Geffen had a production deal with Warner and was a big fan of Rice's books. It wasn't long before he became the latest Hollywood producer to try to turn the material into a film.

Geffen's first step was to throw out all the previous script versions and to return to the source, Rice herself. Hollywood is notorious for not commissioning authors of novels to script the film versions of their work, but Geffen was not a typical Hollywood producer, and sticking to convention was not one of his habits.

Rice was thrilled and jumped at the chance to work on the movie of her book. A forthright and opinionated person, she was not backward in telling Geffen how she thought the transfer should be handled. She even had a series of suggestions for potential directors: David Cronenberg (*The Fly, Dead Ringers*), Ridley Scott (*Alien, Blade Runner*) or Neil Jordan, who had directed the fairy-tale-inspired *Company of Wolves* (1984), a film Rice loved.

Jordan, the Irishman behind a series of low-budget British thrillers such as

Mona Lisa (1986) and the controversial box-office hit *The Crying Game* (1992), had suffered two previously disappointing Hollywood experiences with *High Spirits* (1988) and his remake of *We're No Angels* (1989). On the back of the success of *The Crying Game* Geffen signed him up.

Jordan's first step was to rewrite Rice's script, bringing the film more into tune with his ideas, but alienating Rice. 'The story didn't work – nobody got the script right – so I had to get the script to work, to make it kind of beautiful,' said Jordan, justifying his revision. 'I had to bring the moral dilemma to the forefront, Louis's whole question of is he evil or is he good? Or is he beyond evil?'

The first of several behind-the-scenes production fights began over the screenplay. The final on-screen credit read 'Screenplay by Anne Rice, based on her novel', but only after Writers' Guild arbitration, whose rules indicated that a director and writer must have contributed over 50% original material to the screenplay to justify a credit. Jordan had beefed up the screenplay by injecting more material from Rice's own novels, so his painstaking work on the script was not deemed to be 'original'.

The next battle was over the casting. Neil Jordan was set on having Brad Pitt play the troubled Louis from the beginning: 'I saw everything he'd done and he is just absolutely captivating,' said Jordan. At least this decision seemed to be welcomed by Rice. Then came a flood of suggestions from Rice to Geffen and Jordan of who she would like cast as Lestat. Her suggestions ranged from the ridiculous, like Rutger Hauer, her original model for Lestat in 1976, but now too old to really do the part justice, to Jeremy Irons, John Malkovich, William Baldwin, Ralph Fiennes and Mel Gibson. Jordan had other ideas, and pursued Daniel Day Lewis.

All hell broke loose, however, when Neil Jordan announced his choice of Tom Cruise. 'It's just that the guy is kind of amazing,' Jordan said. 'After Daniel [Day-Lewis] turned it down I made a list and Tom was at the top. I thought, "If he goes the distance, if he could go where his character went, it would be really great."'

Hollywood is no stranger to controversies when strong-willed creators or fans take on producers over the casting of favourite characters. Michael Keaton as *Batman* and Tom Hanks as Sherman McCoy, Bruce Willis as an alcoholic British journalist and Melanie Griffith as McCoy's mistress in *Bonfire of the Vanities* had been the most recent examples. It was no real surprise to Geffen nor Jordan, then, when Rice's fans and even Rice herself began to disapprove volubly of the casting of Cruise. They were surprised, however, by the way in which the controversy became something of a *cause celèbre* in the film press.

In an interview in *The Los Angeles Times* in August 1993 Rice made clear her objections: 'I was particularly stunned by the casting of Cruise. He is no more my vampire Lestat than Edward G. Robinson is Rhett Butler...I'm puzzled as to why Cruise would want to take on the role. He's a cute kid, on top of the world and on his way to becoming a great actor, but I'm not sure he knows what he's getting into...He should do himself a favour and withdraw.'

Cruise, the biggest movie star of his generation, was not about to do any such thing. As far as Geffen and Jordan were concerned, he was capable of playing the role and – almost as important – was a form of box office insurance. The combination of Cruise and Brad Pitt would be enough to ensure that the film could enjoy a healthy opening few weeks.

Louis De Ponte Du Lac is a lost soul, who agrees to be turned into a
vampire so as to end his grief over the deaths of his family.

The casting of Brad as Louis was straightforward, but that of Tom Cruise (right) as his vampire mentor Lestat caused considerable controversy.

Neither Geffen, Jordan nor Cruise were about to rise to Rice's bait, even if she continued to up the ante. At a Halloween rally of her supporters, she continued to vent her frustrations: 'I wanted to call David Geffen and say "How the hell could you do this?"'

Cruise was more measured in his reaction to the controversy: 'She was opposed to me being Lestat based on the other characters that I've played. She had created Lestat and feels great affinity for this character because of her family, her daughter and what occurred. It was very important to her - but it hurt me.'

In fact, Rice felt that Brad Pitt would make a better Lestat than Tom Cruise. After all, Lestat is described in the novel as 'an overpowering person...very tall, very blond, very athletic, very full.' Brad Pitt down to a tee.

'They should have reversed the roles,' confirmed Rice. 'Brad Pitt would have made a wonderful Lestat. He did that wonderful thing with his hips in *Thelma & Louise*, remember that? And *A River Runs Through It*...this is a guy who could play Lestat.'

Rice was right in as much as the role of Lestat was certainly going to be a stretch for Cruise, best known for playing squeaky clean good guys. In *Interview With the Vampire* he would be playing a bitchy, decadent vampire who had to exude sexuality and menace at one and the same time.

Escaping all the controversy was Brad Pitt. He'd received the script for *Interview With the Vampire* at the same time as that for *Legends of the Fall*, and quickly committed to both films, meaning a punishing shooting schedule. His restricted shooting period on *Legends of the Fall* led straight into the filming of *Interview With the Vampire*. He went from the gruelling, physically demanding production in the wide-open spaces of the Canadian countryside, to a largely interior-based, dark, twisted romance. It was something of a dramatic change. 'I did *Legends of the Fall* for four months,' recalled Pitt, 'a very tragic character, very tormented, and this guy's [Louis] even more tormented...'

For David Geffen, Pitt was perfect in the role: 'In *Interview With the Vampire*, Brad's character is very passive. You need an awful lot of charisma to be in a movie where someone else does all the action. And Brad has it.'

Casting was completed with the addition of young actress Kirsten Dunst in the pivotal role of Claudia, the young vampire who eventually teams up with Louis to rid the world of Lestat. Despite achieving the dream of teenagers the world over and getting to kiss Brad Pitt, in interviews Dunst would maintain a distinctly unimpressed facade. Other vampires were played by Jordan regular Stephen Rea and rising Hollywood heart-throb Antonio Banderas.

The problems with *Interview With the Vampire* were not over just yet. Cast in the small, but pivotal role, of the interviewer – the character who talks to Louis in modern-day San Francisco about his vampire life – was rising young actor River

Louis (Pitt) shelters the young girl (Kirsten Dunst) Lestat has turned into a vampire to act as his companion.

Malloy (Christian Slater) interviews Louis about his vampirism in modern San Francisco. Before his death River Phoenix was cast as Malloy.

Phoenix. With a reputation for clean living – Phoenix and his family were New Age-type evangelists for vegetarianism and healthy living – and a dedication to his work, as well as a strong, ever increasing, fan following, Phoenix was the ideal choice.

Tragedy struck at the end of October 1993 when Phoenix collapsed and died outside Johnny Depp's Hollywood nightclub The Viper Room on the corner of Sunset Boulevard and Larabee Street. Declared dead on arrival at hospital, Phoenix's sudden and unexpected death was attributed to a cocktail of drugs. The clean-living myth was blown wide open as stories of Phoenix's drug abuse hit the headlines for months following his death.

Pitt had his own view of drugs in Hollywood, a scene he'd never really been seriously involved in. 'The drug thing is out. I've experimented with all kinds of lifestyles, but you either quit drugs or you die. I'm smart enough to learn from other people's mistakes. River Phoenix was the best of all the young actors. He was getting deeper and deeper into his roles – and then, nothing. His death threw a damper on *Interview With the Vampire*. It woke up a lot of people.'

River Phoenix's death left the producers and director with a problem. They were due to start shooting and were now without an interviewer. Among the replacements mooted were Leonardo DiCaprio and Stephen Dorff, but the role went to Christian Slater, who managed to get six days away from shooting his thriller *Murder in the First* (1994). Slater donated his $250,000 salary to two of Phoenix's favourite environmental charities: Earth Save of Santa Cruz and Earth Trust of Malibu.

Interview With the Vampire finally began its production schedule with 40 days of night shooting near the bayous of Louisiana. The first few days, mainly close-ups of the actors, were scrapped when David Geffen decided the vampire make-up was too heavy. These shots were eventually picked up on a British soundstage where the production team recreated the bayou backdrops.

Production for the studio shot scenes switched to London, with the stars flying over amid something of a media feeding frenzy. Tabloid newshounds and photographers would try every trick under the book to infiltrate the set and snap the much-sought after first photograph of Pitt or Cruise in full vampire regalia. Such was the paranoia that a covered walkway-cum-tunnel was built to cover the route from the dressing rooms to the sets from prying eyes. 'It's not a tunnel, it's a canvas passage,' a publicist helpfully informed the waiting press.

But Jordan's precautions were in vain after a British tabloid paper managed to snap the eagerly awaited photo of Tom Cruise.

Security wasn't the only problem. Making *Interview With the Vampire* was one of the worst experience working on a movie that Brad Pitt had ever endured – not physically, but psychologically.

'I hated doing this movie. Hated it. I loved watching it. Completely hated doing it. My character is depressed from the beginning to the end. Five and a half months of that is too much.'

The security at Pinewood, where the film was being shot, wasn't enough to stop Pitt cruising the streets of Notting Hill, searching out pie restaurants or pubs with good pints of beer and the inevitable journalists to give interviews to. 'I wake up and feel good,' he told Chris Heath of *Empire* magazine, 'and I got to go to work and feel bad. I gotta find a comedy next, man, or I'll break out the razor blades...'

Committed to playing the part – it was too good an opportunity to miss – Pitt didn't manage to overcome his problems on set simply by playing music or sketching as he'd done on films in the past. 'You gotta understand,' he explained, 'My character wants to kill himself for the whole movie. I've never thought about killing myself. It was a sick thing. I don't like it when a movie messes with your day. "You are the devil! We belong in Hell!" Do you know how hard it is to say lines like that?'

As in *Legends of the Fall*, Pitt found himself being subsumed by the character he was playing. The strain of demonstrating the angst experienced by Louis, who sucks the blood from rodents to avoid killing humans, was spilling over into his everyday life, making his stay in London a lonely and tormented one. 'This person is a very reactive role,' said Pitt. 'I understand why women complain a lot about their roles, because that's it right there.'

Part of Pitt's problem was his lack of preparation time for the film. 'I never made it through the book,' he sheepishly admitted.

Neil Jordan was watching his star closely. 'He's never played a part where he has to deal with a huge amount of speech; he's very much played himself. Brad has no technique. He didn't come up through the theatre. He's a movie actor *par excellence*. Louis is a deeply empathetic human being, which is what Brad is. He identified so strongly with the part that halfway through the film, he was having a lot of trouble with his character. He didn't realise it, but he was eating, drinking, sleeping and living that character. Brad is all emotion; Tom plays all aggressive, an individual who's all icy.'

Dealing with the travails of his character was not the only problem Pitt faced.

(Top picture) *Brad Pitt* and Tom Cruise, as rival leads in the film, were wary and distrustful of each other throughout the shooting of *Interview With the Vampire*. (Lower picture) Lestat (Tom Cruise, left) and Louis (Brad Pitt), creatures of the night, feed on a lady of the night.

He also had to cope with the petty jealousies and rivalries of his co-star Tom Cruise, who seemed to feel threatened by Pitt's presence.

Although one of the world's biggest film stars, Tom Cruise has never been renowned for his acting ability and the part of Lestat was regarded as difficult for him, not only by Anne Rice, but by many people involved in and outside of the production. More practically, Cruise was shorter than his six-foot-tall co-star. Rumours emanated from the troubled set that Cruise's voice was proving to be too high, but Cruise himself was felt to be too short to be credible opposite Pitt. Platform boots were quickly ordered up to make the co-stars of more equal stature, according to the rumours. Not so, sources on the production said, claiming that Cruise's period boots, which were merely part of his costume, happened to have the happy side-effect of making him taller.

'You're not going to get me to talk about that,' said costume designer Sandy Powell of the height controversy. Powell was not allowed to retain any of her drawings or sketches from the production for fear that some of five-foot-nine Cruise's secrets might leak out.

Pitt was sanguine about the whole fiasco. 'It's something people want to make a big deal out of. He wanted his character to be more physically dominant. It does make sense...and then, it doesn't.'

That wasn't the end of the problems between the stars though. They may have passed the time recreating Cruise's *Days of Thunder* in go-cart races, which Cruise invariable won, but the rival leads were wary and mistrustful of each other. They had been forced together on this movie by the logic of Hollywood packaging deals, but they were rivals for the same crown and they both knew it.

'You gotta understand, Tom and I are...we walk in different directions,' claimed Pitt of their on-set rivalries. 'He's North Pole. I'm South. He's coming at you with a handshake, whereas I may bump into you, I may not. Y'know.'

In the 90s, Pitt's laid-back sex appeal was surpassing the aggressive, controlled and calculated star image crafted carefully by Cruise throughout the 80s. Faced with the rival who was chasing his tail, it seems clear that Cruise forgot some of the usual niceties of star communication. Stories of bitching on the set and hours spent comparing trailer sizes and privileges leaked to the waiting, hungry press from Pinewood like water through a sieve.

'I always thought there was this underlying competition that got in the way of any real conversation,' was how Pitt summed up the situation afterwards, putting a diplomatic gloss on his childish spats with Cruise. 'It wasn't nasty by any means, not at all. But it was just there, and it bugged me a bit. But I tell you, he catches a lot of shit because he's on top, but he is a good actor and he advances in this film. He did it. I mean, you have to respect that.'

Cruise was generous about Pitt's acting ability, pinning down the secret of the actor's success: 'His emotions are all right there on the surface.'

The battle royale between the stars was only the last in a long line of troubles that had dogged *Interview With the Vampire* for over 18 years. Thankfully, there was a silver lining when near the end of post-production a videotape of the film was sent off to Anne Rice to solicit her opinion. The result was double page advertising spreads in *The Los Angeles Times*, *The New York Times* and Hollywood's in-house newspaper, *Variety*, in the form of an open letter from Anne Rice declaring how much she actually appreciated the movie. 'I loved the film from start to finish, and

Kirsten Dunst, who played Louis's young female companion Claudia, was one teenager unmoved by kissing Brad Pitt.

I found myself deeply impressed by every aspect of its making...The charm, the humour and the invincible innocence of my beloved hero Lestat are all alive in Tom Cruise's courageous performance; the guilt and suffering of Louis are poignantly portrayed by Brad Pitt...I think you will embrace this film as I do...See this film, guys, see it!'

It was quite a dramatic about-face after Rice's earlier vehement statements about what she saw as horrendous mis-casting. The cost of placing the advertisements would be pretty close to $100,000. All suggestions that Hollywood commerce had won out and that Anne Rice had been in receipt of a not inconsiderable sum of money to endorse the film were all rejected out of hand by all parties as false and malicious.

David Geffen was well pleased with Anne Rice's Road-to-Damascus-like conversion to the film version of her work: 'The movie and the performances were beyond her wildest expectations. She thought Tom was incredible.' The next test to be faced by the film would be the international press critics.

Neil Jordan was particularly concerned with how the critics would react to his film. He had more to worry about than most film-makers. Anne Rice's earlier intervention in the production of the film had been widely noticed, perhaps even more so than the pages proclaiming her support for the film. 'I think it damaged the critics' reaction,' said Jordan of Rice's first batch of publicity, 'because there had been so much public talk about it. It won't affect the audiences. She said the movie was great. She didn't say "I'm sorry," though.'

The critics were reserved. David Denby in *New York* magazine found the film 'boring...and remote', while *Rolling Stone* was 'Dazzled, but unmoved', and *The New Yorker* claimed that Jordan's 'virtuosity cannot hide the movie's emptiness'.

British critics were less harsh but here ambivalent about the performances of both Tom Cruise and particularly Brad Pitt. According to *The Daily Mail*, 'Pitt remains a whining, monotonous killjoy...', while *The Sunday Express* felt 'Brad, as the reluctant bloodsucker Louis...is far more suited to the role of scrubbed sexual magnet in more gentle films such as *A River Runs Through It*...' Other publications were kinder. According to *The Independent*, 'Brad Pitt wanders the centuries looking elegant and melancholy, which is a relatively easy task given that vampirism in this version isn't disturbing.' *The Guardian* pegged Pitt's Louis as 'far from a grim cardboard cut-out. [Cruise] is more than equalled by Pitt, who tells his story of descent into hell...'

Interview With the Vampire opened at cinemas shortly before *Legends of the Fall*, and together the films were make-or-break time for Brad Pitt. Their fate was now out of his control. All he could do now was sit back and wait, relax and have some fun with Yit while reading new scripts. His intention now was to find something less taxing, something lighter that would allow him to relax a bit during the shoot, something that would be based closer to home.

Offers came which he declined, such as a starring role in a film being developed by James Cameron entitled *The Crowded Room*, based on a true tale of someone who suffers multiple personalities. More high-profile was the chance to star as a lawyer in a big-budget version of John Grisham's thriller, *The Chamber*. His character would be defending an ageing racist killer incarcerated on Death Row. Pitt went for the role but then pulled out when the original director, Ron Howard, left the production. In its place he considered going the swashbuckling route in a remake of *Captain Blood* for Chuck Russell, director of *The Mask* (1994).

Instead, he spent time at home, enjoying the tranquillity of not having to subsume himself in another character. For a while Pitt got to be himself. Every so often he'd head downtown, to a club like the Luna Park, perhaps to see his actor friend Dermot Mulroney's band The Sweet and Low Orchestra play a gig. Mulroney and Pitt would hang out afterwards, shooting the breeze, discussing Mulroney's recent trips to Europe.

Before embarking on a new film, though, Pitt found himself living alone again. Rumours of a dalliance with actress Thandie Newton on the set of *Interview With the Vampire* had reached Yit, the final straw in a relationship that was never that strong to begin with. Tired of Pitt's constant absences and the tales of yet another film-making romance, Yit packed up her bobcats and moved right back out. For Pitt it had been brief, but fun. After Juliette Lewis he was not ready for and was not looking for another head-over-heels long-term romance. He felt free to play the field and see what came along. After all, if the two films about to unspool at cinemas around the world were hits, he would be spoilt for choice.

Interview With the Vampire allowed Brad to hone the riding skills he had learned for *Legends of the Fall*.

10 Sin and Redemption

THE PUBLIC voted on *Interview With the Vampire* by buying tickets to cinemas, with the film taking $38.7 million over its first weekend. The film was placed fifth on *Variety*'s list of all-time biggest openings though by the end of its run, the movie was expected not to gross much more than a very respectable $110. *Legends of the Fall* was even more successful. It was the number one film at the American box office for four straight weeks, taking in excess of $60 million during that period. The first big hit of 1995, it eliminated any remaining doubts about Pitt's ability to successfully tackle a leading role and open a big-budget drama. Its success according to Lynn Snowden in American *Premiere* magazine, was 'thanks almost entirely to Pitt's sex appeal…'.'

Brad Pitt could now feel that he had made it. He'd been around in Hollywood for just over eight years and had climbed the slippery slope from dressing as a chicken on the streets of LA through low-budget cult movies like *Johnny Suede*, *Cool World* and *Kalifornia*. Now he'd arrived at the destination he'd set out for: Hollywood's A-list. With the box office successes of *Interview With the Vampire* and *Legends of the Fall*, he was now first choice for many of the most high profile roles in town.

Now he was in that position, he could be choosy about what he committed to. He didn't have to be constantly in work, he was financially secure. The only real consideration was to build solidly on the success he'd achieved, to be careful to maintain his bankability and at all costs avoid a flop movie.

With that in mind he passed on many of the films offered to him. The dross he dismissed out of hand, but some high-profile films were also rejected. *Model Daughter*, a comedy about a divorcing couple fighting for their child's love, would have allowed him to explore a more emotional character than he'd attempted before, but he turned it down.

Pitt struck up a friendship with Ben Stiller, a young writer-director he felt a strong bond with. Stiller had enjoyed a modicum of success with *Reality Bites* (1995), a Generation X comedy-drama starring Johnny Depp's ex-girlfriend Winona Ryder. The young director was planning a film about the Rolling Stones which piqued Pitt's interest, as he'd got into their music through his relationship with Yit. It says much for his new star power that his interest alone was enough to put the film into development and his later withdrawal was enough to cause the project to be quickly scrapped.

Politics beckoned in *City Hall*, a drama about political corruption in New York, which also passed across Pitt's desk. The film was eventually made with John Cusack (in what would have been Pitt's role), Al Pacino and Bridget Fonda. He considered other options, like an action movie. A side-step to action hero territory was a well-worn method of enjoying some variety and still staying at the top of the Hollywood tree. It had worked for Keanu Reeves in *Speed* (1994), but it wasn't a route that attracted Pitt, so he opted out of *Tears of the Sun*, an adventure set in the Amazon rainforest to be directed by John Woo. He was more interested in character-based parts than muscle-based ones. Crime and punishment didn't appeal either, so *Last Dance* had to find another star.

One role Pitt did take up was on audio tape, not film. He recorded the audio book version of *The Crossing* by Cormac McCarthy. Although he didn't read a great deal, he considered McCarthy his favourite novelist. According to *People* he was the ideal person to have tackled the book. '[His] twangy stoicism perfectly reflects the novel's tone.'

Making a decision about what to do next became a problem. He had to make the right choice. Doubt about the likely fate of the finished film prompted him to follow Mel Gibson in turning down the lead role in *The Saint*. To those around him, his advisors and agents, maintaining their client's new-found bankability became the main object of their concentration.

That bankability was ensured when in January 1995 *People* magazine named Pitt the 'Sexiest Man Alive'. The accolade brought acres of good publicity, but it also confirmed him as public property. 'I think that was a cruel thing to do to me,' said Pitt of the award. 'It was some cruel and heinous joke. A friend of mine said they misspelled it – it was supposed to be the "Sexiest Moron"!' *Speed* star Sandra Bullock was named Sexiest Woman.

Later in the year he was to be annointed with an altogether different label: one of the world's smelliest stars. Along with Keanu Reeves, Pitt was dubbed one of tinseltown's 'hygenically challenged'. A London tabloid claimed that he was tired of being fussed over by make-up and wardrobe people on shoots and often went for days off-camera without changing his clothes. Apparently, Pitt followed this charge with a shopping spree, spending $1,000 on Clavin Klein underwear, suggesting that he thought the paper might have a point.

Contemplating future roles, Pitt also had other considerations in mind, remembering his gruelling schedule on his last two films, as well as the heavy emotions he'd had to deal with. 'Right now I'd like to play a guy who just wants to fuck everybody so I can have a damn good time,' he claimed.

He was looking for something more uplifting than *Interview With the Vampire* and something less physically taxing than *Legends of the Fall*. He was also having doubts about his own abilities to carry strong emotions on the screen. During the making of *Interview With the Vampire*, the mother of one of the workers on the set had died. 'I was thinking, we do death every other day in the movies, you know, but you'll never be able to do it to the full impact of what it is to have someone die. It's pretty much bullshit, really, what we do. I was sitting there on the set and someone was dying in front of me, and I was supposed to be tormented by it, and I'd see him – the person whose mother died – and he was going through something much more, and I felt like a phoney.'

From now on he couldn't afford to fail, and merely impressing or surprising the audience with the revelation that the pretty boy can actually act was not going to be good enough either. 'I'm smart enough to know that this is the start, and I'm also smart enough to know that this is the end of surprising people. From now on it's expected of me.'

However, his next move was surprising, turning down one of the leading roles in the true-life space-age thriller *Apollo 13* (1995) opposite Tom Hanks, instead signing on to star in a new low-budget thriller called *Seven*.

'The script had been around for over four years,' Pitt said of *Seven*. 'At first description, I thought it was just another cop-buddy flick, but upon reading it, I knew it was different. People are going to love it or hate it, but they'll be talking about it.'

Andrew Kevin Walker was the man who had put the words down on paper. The 31-year-old from Pennsylvania concocted his devilish mix of *film noir* and horror shocker while working in New York City.

'I lived there for about five years,' he said of New York. 'I was miserable just about every minute of every day. I just couldn't adjust to living in a big, angry, loud city. It was a reaction to that. New York is an amazing place, but it's a cauldron of unpleasantries. You see it everywhere from the projects and parks to the subways and street corners. I was working for a low-budget film company that made exploitation horror films. The seven deadly sins seemed easily encapsulated.'

Walker had previously scripted the Jeff Goldblum thriller *Hideaway* (1995), based on a Dean R. Koontz novel, and *Brainscan* (1994), an ultra-low-budget flick about a killer computer game. He put together his screenplay for *Seven* over a six-month period in 1991. 'It by-passed a lot of the bigger studios, probably because the subject matter was too dark.'

Seven is about as dark as they come in mainstream, star-driven cinema. Initially seeming to be a police procedural thriller, the latter third of the film turns into a psychological horror film, focused on Pitt's character.

Pitt was cast as Detective David Mills, an ambitious, keen-as-mustard young detective who has secured a posting to the big city. Born and raised in the country,

Obsessed with his own self-image, Detective Mills fails to make real contact with the older Lieutenant Somerset, unlike his wife who wants to get to know the person, in *Seven*.

like his beautiful young wife (Gwyneth Paltrow), he feels out of place in the city, but is determined to make a success of his opportunity. He's partnered with Lieutenant William Somerset (Morgan Freeman), a philosophical old timer who is one week away from retirement. Having tired of fighting a losing battle against the tide of crime on the streets, Somerset is looking forward to turning in his badge and gun in order to move out to the country.

During the week that the film covers, Somerset and Mills investigate a series of bizarre and gruesome murders, each one of which is labelled by the murderer with one of the seven deadly sins. Despite the illicit help of FBI moles, the pair are not able to crack the case, until John Doe (played by *The Usual Suspects* star Kevin Spacey in what was a surprise cameo) walks into the station and gives himself up. It's then that the real descent into horror begins for Mills.

After by-passing the major studios, Andrew Kevin Walker's script for *Seven* came into the hands of producer Arnold Kopelson, responsible for such films as Oliver Stone's *Platoon* (1986), the big-screen remake of *The Fugitive* (1994) inspired by the 60s TV series, and *Falling Down* (1994), a controversial portrait of life in modern Los Angeles that starred Michael Douglas.

'I grew up in Brooklyn and rode the subways. I saw danger every day of my life. This was a script that was so brilliantly conceived, it grabbed me and shook me. Very few writers have been able to do that,' recalled Kopelson.

Kopelson approached David Fincher to persuade him to direct. Fincher, a graduate of the music video industry, had withdrawn from film-making after a bruising experience making the third in the *Alien* series.

Alien3 was his first feature film and he had jumped at the chance to make it. The problem was that he inherited a script that had been through so many hands that it had become an incoherent blend of drafts and treatments compiled by such luminaries as SF writer and cyberpunk godfather William Gibson and acclaimed New Zealand film-maker Vincent Ward. The responsibility of maintaining a hit series of films was also a daunting task. Heavily criticised upon release, *Alien3* has aged better than most critics in 1992 expected. His dark take on the *Alien* saga is reflected in *Seven*, but this time out, Fincher had total creative control and a cracking script to work with.

'I didn't know what was going to happen at the end,' he said of his first reading the script. 'I liked the fact that the movie was so ruthless. All of a sudden it took this turn and I found myself getting more and more trapped in this kind of evil, and although I felt uncomfortable about being there, I had to keep going...'

Fincher knew that if he could capture even a fraction of that spine-tingling frisson on screen, he'd have a film the likes of which had not been seen since the mid-1970s release of *The Exorcist*. First, though, he had to fight with the producer over the film's bleak ending.

'I called my agent and said "This movie, are they going to make this? I mean, have you read this thing?" and he said, "Yeah, I read it,"' Fincher told *Empire* magazine. 'And I said, "There's this fucking head in the box at the end, it's just amazing. Are they really going to do this?" And he said, "No, you've got the wrong draft." So they sent me the right draft, and it had this big chase at the end to get to the bathroom where the wife is taking a shower and the serial killer's crawling through the window...'

The pat Hollywood version was not the one Fincher wanted to make. He was

Pitt is cast as the novice detective David Mills who thinks he has little to learn from the about-to-retire Lieutenant William Somerset (Morgan Freeman).

The atmosphere of *Seven* is predominantly claustrophobic and threatening.

keen to make the original draft of the script, the head-in-the-box ending, even though he thought he'd never get away with it. He was due for a surprise. 'I went to talk to Michael [De Luca, New Line head of production] and said "The head-in-the box, that's the cool ending," and he said, "Yeah, I thought so too, let's go make that version".'

Serial killer movies were ten-a-penny in the 1990s, but no one had seen a film as gritty and downright nasty as *Seven* in a long time. One reason such films weren't being made was that since the heyday of the pre-*Star Wars* mid-70s American cinema, producers, directors and stars had become more and more unwilling to take risks with the audience, with the narrative and with their own public images.

For Pitt, the chance to change his image, lop off his long hair and play a cop who doesn't enjoy a happy ending was too good to pass by: 'You have to find something you are interested in, so you'll bring some truth to it. It may be interesting to me, but I don't know if it's going to be interesting to others. I have a vision going in of what I'm after. Then I look at how I end up once it's done. I think we got what I was looking for in *Seven*.'

While Morgan Freeman was easily cast by David Fincher as Somerset, the older cop, he didn't have a clear idea of who could play Mills. He needed someone who could not only draw an audience, but was also able to handle the drama of the role, and who could be afforded within his overall budget of $20 million. Brad Pitt was not his first choice, as he felt that the role required a more grungy, down-to-earth presence than Pitt seemed to offer.

An accident Pitt sustained to his hand in shooting *Seven* adds to David Mills's
appearance of vulnerability in the closing stages of the film.

Mills and Somerset investigate another murder labelled by the killer as the punishment for one of the Seven Deadly Sins.

Informed of Pitt's interest in the script, though, Fincher was only too happy to meet with the young star, well aware of his marquee value. The pair had lunch and Fincher discovered that Pitt was as wildly enthusiastic about the film – and the head-in-the-box ending – as Fincher himself was.

'He was incredibly enthusiastic,' Fincher recalled, 'and I told him, "This is not a major thing. This is a minor movie for everyone involved – and that's how we've got to keep looking at it. It's a little, tiny, minor movie..." and he was like, "I'm in. I want to do it".'

'Brad helped to get the movie made,' Michael De Luca admitted. 'When he came aboard, people got a lot less insecure about the film. It was very brave of him. I love when people go against type. To come off pictures like *Legends of the Fall* and *Interview With the Vampire* and play a homophobic, bigoted, neo-fascistic cop with a crew cut – it was a very cool thing for Brad to do.'

Although his character is put through the mill by the end of the film, part of the attraction for Pitt was playing someone more down to earth and ordinary than either Tristan Ludlow in *Legends of the Fall*, who was a force of nature incarnated as a man, or the morose reluctant vampire Louis in *Interview with the Vampire*. 'Cop chasing a bad guy – complete genre. I figured I'd give that a try. The guy's got no problems, that's the key thing,' admitted Pitt. 'Just have some fun. Just see if I can say those lines, get the killer...'

After casting Pitt, Fincher's next problem was finding an actress who could play the part of the young cop's wife. He required someone who could hold her own opposite 'the world's Sexist Man' and garner a great deal of audience sympathy during her brief time on screen – sympathy that was required to make the climax of

Brad at the London premiere of *Legends of the Fall*, after finishing *Seven*.

the film work to its full effect. It was a tall order, and Fincher saw over 100 candidates.

His first choice was Gwyneth Paltrow, having seen her in the little-known film *Flesh and Bone* (1995). Pitt had also recommended the actress, whom he'd met casually through a mutual friend a few months earlier. He'd also remembered her auditioning for the Julia Ormond role in *Legends of the Fall*. Fincher, however, felt the chances of her accepting the role he had to offer were slim to non-existent, a feeling reinforced by those around him.

'She was my first choice, and everybody said "You'll never get her – she's too picky, she doesn't want to play the cop's wife, she's not interested in doing this stuff, this is too dark." Finally Brad called her and asked her to come in, not to read, but to meet, and I remember telling Arnold [Kopelson, producer] to watch this girl. He hadn't seen *Flesh and Bone* and she came in and sat down for about two seconds and said, "Do you have a rest room?" and she walked into the rest room and closed the door and Arnold said, "She's perfect..."'

In being instrumental in engineering Paltrow's casting in *Seven* Pitt was unknowingly giving her a large role too in his private life. When time came for the pair to work together in December 1994, it was clear that there was something between them was much deeper than what was required for screen husband-and-wife. It was clear to those around them, too.

'The chemistry between them was real,' according to Morgan Freeman. 'I've always been floored by [her mother] Blythe Danner. And here she comes – she had the gift.' But he didn't see Paltrow throwing the young actor off his laid-back stride. 'He's a real settled young man, considering the whirlwind that goes around him. As

Gwyneth Paltrow plays Detective Mills's beautiful but essentially homely young wife, recently moved to the big city from the country.

The casting of Gwyneth Paltrow as Pitt's on-screen wife quickly led to a real romance. Their relationship went public at the British premiere of *Legends of the Fall*.

Brad and Gwyneth after a David Bowie concert.

far as you can tell with anyone, he's calm like the eye of the storm...'

Both Gwyneth Paltrow's parents work in the media. In addition to her actress mother, her father is TV producer Bruce Paltrow, the man behind hospital drama *St Elsewhere*. As well as her part in *Flesh and Bone* alongside Meg Ryan and Dennis Quaid, Paltrow had appeared as Thomas Jefferson's daughter in *Jefferson in Paris* (1995). She'd previously dated actor Robert Sean Leonard (*Dead Poets Society*, 1989) and Donovan Leitch, Pitt's co-star in his early film *Cutting Class*. Aged only 22 when she took the role in *Seven*, Paltrow was almost ten years younger than her co-star. That fact didn't put off Pitt, although it had been one of the reasons for the end of his relationship with Juliette Lewis – maybe he'd finally grown up himself. 'It was love at first sight, as far as I was concerned,' said Pitt.

Overcoming the publicity that surrounded Pitt, Paltrow was able to put aside any intimidation she may have felt at getting involved with him. 'I don't know who that Brad Pitt is,' she said of the *People* magazine label. 'I know a very grounded, peaceful and wise person. And besides, he has three dogs. People who have dogs are usually good!'

Producer Arnold Kopelson noted the attraction that built between the two stars on the set of *Seven*. 'They are very much in love. The chemistry between them is obvious. Gwyneth is very confident. She is a strong woman who is not threatened by the attention that Brad gets.'

'It was love at second sight,' said Paltrow, modifying Pitt's claim and recalling her previous meeting with her new partner. 'When I was 15 I saw *Thelma & Louise*, and I thought "Who is that gorgeous guy?" And years later, here I am living my dream. I don't think either of us was expecting love or looking for it and it came as a shock to both of us. We went to an Italian restaurant in Los Angeles for a wonderful meal and the romance grew from there. I was charmed by his intelligence and sensitivity, his closeness to his family and the way in which he was completely down to earth.'

Acting the part of Mills's wife became an easy call for Paltrow, who simply acted out the feelings that the pair were really developing for each other. 'The scenes were really sexy and sweet. I mean, it's not hard kissing Brad, so I had a lot of fun.'

While the romance developed, the pair still had a film to shoot. To make their roles as convincing as possible Pitt and Freeman undertook a depth of research neither had tackled on any film before. During pre-production the unlikely pair were taught in the ways of the modern, urban police force by Sergeant Ed Arneson. 'It's our job to make them look as realistic as possible,' said Arneson. 'If they come across as real policemen who have handled weapons their whole careers, are fluid in their motions, and talk like real policemen, then we've done our job.'

For Pitt this process involved firearms training. 'He was very receptive to our input,' recalled Arneson. 'He focused on tactics, and his intensive training will come across looking quite realistic on screen.'

Pitt was no stranger to guns, having grown up around them in Missouri and never having been without one all the time he'd been living in Los Angeles. 'I grew up with firearms, more shotguns and rifles than handguns. But I hung out with some detectives who took me around and taught me a little respect for their job. They taught me how to deal with handguns, clearing corners, what your focus is on in order not to get shot. These guys have a hairy job.'

When he was a teenager, Pitt's father had taught him how to use weapons. It was simply part of life in the South – guns were not seen as unusual or out of the ordinary. The habit of having a gun around stayed with Pitt in the urban jungle of Los Angeles. Unapologetically stored at his Hollywood home are two 12 gauge shotguns and a handgun. While hoping he'll never have to use the weapons, he seems prepared to if he has to, according to an interview in *Rolling Stone*. 'Damn right, if someone comes into my house in the middle of the night, I'm going to shoot.'

Seven's look was dictated by Pitt's availability. Although he had wanted to take a back seat, Pitt found himself capitalising on his current position to secure further work, and he agreed to appear in a featured role in a new film to be directed by Terry Gilliam. The schedules meant he had a short period of time in which to wrap *Seven*.

As a result, according to Fincher, the film's rain-soaked atmosphere came about because of 'a pragmatic decision based on the fact that we had Brad Pitt for 55 days and then he was going on to Terry Gilliam's movie [*Twelve Monkeys*] – there were no ifs, ands or buts about it. So, it was raining in LA at the time and we knew we'd have to match in the exteriors stuff that was being shot as interiors. Also, it was a way to kind of make it not look like Los Angeles, 'cause Los Angeles is always seen in the sun.'

Much of the work had to be completed in a rush. That led to people getting careless – prime among them was Pitt himself, who suffered an injury during the filming of the movie's central chase scene. 'I was running across the tops of the cars in the rain, and I went through a window and cut all along my forearm. I'm looking at bones in my arm that you're not supposed to see,' he recalled. 'I cut one tendon, I abraded another and I cut some nerves. I didn't even think of that when I first saw

The two policemen are constantly taunted by the mysterious serial killer in *Seven*, even when they think they have tracked him down.

it. It's pretty good now, though. I've got almost all the feeling back, but not quite.' Pitt hoped that his accident would have been caught by the camera and could be used in the film, but it wasn't to be. He fell over out of the camera's sights, but not out of earshot: 'They missed it, the bastards. But I could hear it. I went ass first.' The accident and injury meant on-the-spot script changes, putting Mills's arm in a sling for the rest of the film. The rest of the production was managed without further incident.

The moral context of the film – or rather the lack of a clear moral direction – was criticised by some people when *Seven* was released, but to the director and his cast they were reflecting life as it is. Fincher saw a message in the film: 'It's the context for the ideas in the movie that are important. It builds and lulls you into thinking there is some kind of sense and order to things. And then the final act of the movie is revealed to contain just as much chaos as everyday life. That's a horrifying realisation for an audience. It compromises their expectations of entertainment...'

Fincher is the first to admit that although he tried to capture true horror, real life has a nasty habit of constantly outdoing cinema: 'I think it's true that evil both attracts and repulses, and I think the film has a lot of evil in it. We live in a society where the most drama people have in their lives is from other people's tragedy. The film really plays on that, and punishes it, too. But there's nothing in it that's more disturbing than those two kids beating a baby to death on a train track. There's nothing in it that's as horrifying as a husband and wife who have been videotaping, raping and killing girls for years. Truth is now always more horrifying than fiction...'

For his part, Brad Pitt agreed with his director: 'I don't see anything more in this film than I see in the news everyday, as far as violence goes. It's more about the telling of the story and then your mind goes from there. This film is a thinker. Listen, I admit it's sick. It's cruel and it's brutal, but it's brutally honest. I think there's a fascination with an understanding of that, and I actually think the film is smart about it. The film doesn't justify the killer's actions by any means, but the guy has got a point...'

For Morgan Freeman, the moral debate was surplus to the purpose of the movie: 'I don't want the audience to get a message. I just want them to get their money's worth.'

With both Fincher and Pitt expecting *Seven* to be a 'small' thriller, they were bowled over by the positive critical reception and the even more surprising response from the public. Producer Arnold Kopelson knew he was on to a good thing, but even he wasn't expecting particularly big things. 'People will see a new Brad Pitt,' he warned before the film was released. 'This movie is a risk because a lot of people are going to hate it, but it won't be ignored. It cost $20 million to make, not a lot by today's standards.'

The film certainly wasn't ignored upon its autumn 1995 release in the United States, and Kopelson need not have been preparing himself for a hostile reception. An opening weekend gross of $14.5 million in mid-September 1995 eclipsed the $8.5 million taken at the same time by Paul Verhoeven's hyped sleaze-fest *Showgirls*. By Christmas *Seven* had grossed over $84 million at the American box office alone, four times what the film had cost to make.

Although many critics felt some of the after-the-fact murder scenes were hard to take, they recognised an exceptional film when they saw one. 'Focus and film craft make *Seven* difficult to dismiss,' said Mike Clark in *USA Today*, while Michael Medved (author of the book *Hollywood versus America* that blames the movies for many of America's social problems) wrote in *The New York Post* that 'Both actors bring considerably more feeling to their characters than you might expect.' CNN's Carol Buckland commented: 'Brad Pitt comes on strong as the young cop. He goes a long, long way toward scuzzing up the glamour boy image. His hair is shorn, his face is stubbled and scratched. Pitt does bring a lot of interesting quirks to his character. He's almost always interesting to watch...even if he's half-obscured by murky shadows!'

The film was welcomed internationally too, seen as a throwback to a gritty, 1970s style of film making. *Sight and Sound* in Britain picked up on the literary references that run through the film, including Dante, Chaucer, Thomas Aquinas and Shakespeare. *Empire's* cover line declared it the 'scariest film every made'. '*Seven* isn't just a movie, it's a psychological trip through hell that leaves your head spinning. Not since *The Exorcist* has there been a mainstream Hollywood movie as extraordinarily dark, bleak, intense and monumentally scary as this. *Seven* goes for the gut...it never lets up. For the ending alone, this is simply unmissable,' wrote Mark Salisbury.

The continuing re-invention of Brad Pitt was noticed by many critics, who saw *Seven* as another step in the actors move towards becoming a leading man in mainstream cinema. 'It is the combination of Brad Pitt and Morgan Freeman that accounts for its success,' said Derek Malcolm in *The Guardian*, while Andrew Preston in *The Daily Express* felt that 'Brad Pitt is at his best ever...' Geoff Brown in *The Times* thought that 'Pitt bounces around, eager for the fray,' as if the actor was exorcising the imposed stillness he had to display in *Interview With the Vampire*.

The critical reaction afforded *Seven* was welcome enough, but it was the audience who made the film a success by parting with their dollars and pounds in huge amounts to see the film. While Pitt had shared the screen with Tom Cruise in *Interview With the Vampire* and with Anthony Hopkins in *Legends of the Fall*, it was he who was the prime attraction for many of the people who went to see the movie. As well as confirming his position in the Hollywood pecking order, *Seven* also allowed director David Fincher to overcome the stigma that had been attached to him since the debacle of *Alien3*.

Although appreciative of good reviews, Pitt is not fond of the press and journalists. He understands the Faustian pact between movie stars and the movie magazines, but that doesn't make him comfortable with it. He is happy enough to talk about his work, but does not enjoy seeing things in print on his private life. 'How do I feel about reading that kinda stuff? It really depends on the day. Sometimes I laugh, other days I just pull down the shades and ignore it. I don't know why it happens. I guess people just want to twist things and hear the negative version.'

'The truth is I don't want people to know me,' Pitt has admitted. 'I don't know a thing about my favourite actors. I don't think you should – they become personalities. It seems to me that it would be better if they didn't know who you were. Then your character would be more believable. I don't know shit about Robert Duvall or John Malkovich, and they're my favourites...'

He has never liked the whole teen idol thing that has dogged his career. 'The thing about these articles,' he said of the teen magazine profiles and features, 'I sit down and give my life views, and it sounds like I'm walking around like a prophet. That's not true, 'cause most of the time I'm out cutting up and laughing and speeding in my car and whatever, whatever, whatever. Yelling at the TV and cranking the tunes...It's like "What's your favourite colour?" I don't know. I like a bunch of 'em.'

The attention of the fans got to be too much when a Hollywood bus tour company began running coach loads past his LA home on Sunday mornings. 'I started lofting eggs at them,' said Pitt, 'I thought that was fair. I'm, like, as open as the next guy, but when freaky people turn up at your home, it's like, Whoah! Get off the train.' Pitt was even the subject of a 'Dear Brad' site on the Internet where fans would leave letters to the star to be read by the public and Pitt himself, should he care to browse the Web. Most of the notes seemed to be from teenage girls declaring their undying love and their hatred of Paltrow. One example was typical: 'I'm Stacy and I really love you. I even have your poster on my wall and you are always looking at me. I know you love me and we are meant to be. So look me up sometime, and please, please, please write back soon. I love you always and forever.' It's hardly surprising Pitt was minded to throw eggs at people.

It wasn't only female fans, either. Pitt discovered his attraction extended to the gay community too, placing him top of a 'Twenty Sexiest Men' readers' poll in British gay magazine *Attitude*, followed closely on the list by Keanu Reeves and

Johnny Depp. Questions were put about his sexuality, according to Juliette Lewis: 'The gay rumour goes wild – for everyone. Like with Leo [DiCaprio], he was like, "Is Brad gay?" And I said, "Leo, you're gay, don't you know? Haven't you heard?".'

Ironically, Pitt was offered the role of a baseball player haunted by a psychotic fan stalker in *The Fan*. Producer Wendy Finerman (*Forrest Gump*, 1994) gave Pitt the script, but he expressed more interest in playing the character of the fan than the star, the latter role being too close to real life for comfort. The film was made in 1995 with Wesley Snipes as the ball player and Robert DeNiro as the fanatic.

In April 1995 Brad Pitt's new relationship became public when he and Paltrow attended the British premiere of *Legends of the Fall* in London. The couple attended the charity premiere at a Leicester Square cinema, in the presence of Prince Charles, at a screening that raised over £100,000 for the Prince's Trust charity. The media, however, were far more interested in the relationship between Paltrow and the 'Sexiest Man Alive'. Pitt's comment to waiting reporters was pithy: 'I've never been happier.'

The pursuit, however, was on. Realising they had a new hot Hollywood couple to rival the on-again, off-again, on-screen, off-screen romances of Johnny Depp and Winona Ryder and Tom Cruise and Nicole Kidman, the media pulled out all the stops to scoop exclusive snapshots of the new star couple.

Following their trip to London, and before Pitt had to return to Los Angeles to take up his role in Terry Gilliam's *Twelve Monkeys*, the couple took the opportunity of a holiday break on the exclusive Caribbean island of St Barts. Thinking themselves to be in a secluded spot, they spent time around their pool naked. The problem was they weren't alone. An enterprising French photographer spotted them and saw a chance to make some money.

His colour full-length shots of Pitt and Paltrow naked were first published by a French magazine, before being reproduced by a British tabloid, and finally ending up on display internationally on the Internet.

Pitt and Paltrow were mortified to discover that their private moments were being splashed all over downmarket publications for public consumption. 'It's pathetic that anything we do is news,' said Paltrow. 'I hate my privacy being invaded, especially since most of it is happening because of who I go out with. It hasn't anything to do with me or my career.' Paltrow called the British tabloid journalists, 'the most hideous creatures on the face of the Earth. It made me recede,' she said of the incident, 'because there are few people I can hang out with. There are few people I feel I can trust.'

Pitt was equally stung by his unintentional public nude scene: 'It was horrendous. It bothers me that they take pictures of these private, special moments and flash semi-naked pictures of my girlfriend. I see how it hurts her.' Pitt started a legal action against the photographer, the photo agency that handled the sale and two French publications. 'I wonder about the rights of privacy,' he said after his actions had begun, trying to play down the impact of the publication of the photos. 'I mean, it all ends up in the litter box anyway.' Pitt avoided pursuing the British tabloids as, unlike France, Britain does not recognise any easily enforceable right of privacy, especially for high-profile celebrities.

Back in Los Angeles after the tabloid tiff, Pitt had business to attend to. He was due to report to the set in Philadelphia of Terry Gilliam's *Twelve Monkeys*, in which he

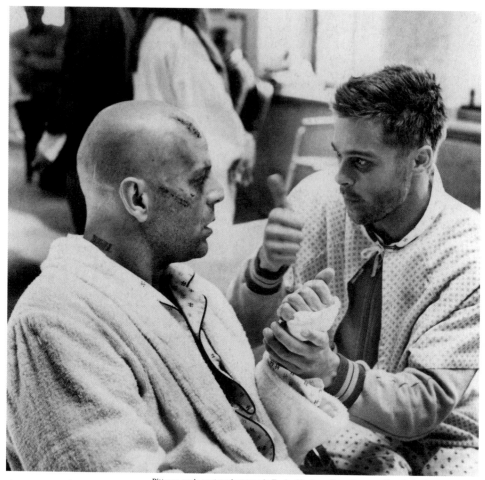

Pitt was again cast against type in Twelve Monkeys, foregoing a macho role for the motormouth
lunatic Jeffrey Goines against Bruce Willis's James Cole.

was co-starring alongside action star Bruce Willis. Gilliam, one-time animator and actor in the *Monty Python* team, had carved out a distinctive visual style in a series of feature films including *Jabberwocky* (1977), *Time Bandits* (1981), *Brazil* (1985), *The Adventures of Baron Munchausen* (1989) and *The Fisher King* (1991). Known as something of a maverick in the Hollywood community, Gilliam had never made blockbusters and some of his movies – particularly *Brazil* and *Baron Munchausen* – had fallen foul of studio interference.

The Fisher King, a fantasy starring Robin William and Jeff Bridges, had restored his reputation somewhat, but it was still another four years before he got underway with *Twelve Monkeys*. In the intermediate years he'd tried to float several projects, including remakes of *A Tale of Two Cities* and *A Connecticut Yankee in King Arthur's Court,* and a film written by Richard LaGravenese, scripter of *The Fisher King*. A long-mooted adaptation of Alan Moore and Dave

Gibbon's graphic novel *Watchmen* had also fallen by the wayside. When offered the script for *Twelve Monkeys*, a feature-length version of a 1962 surreal short called *La Jetée* by Chris Marker, written by David Webb Peoples (*Blade Runner*, 1982, *Unforgiven*, 1992) and his wife Janet Peoples, Gilliam jumped at it.

'I love the idea of trying to alter perceptions and shake people up and make them look at the world in a way they're not used to looking at it,' said Gilliam. 'I found it to be an intriguing and intelligent script. The story is disconcerting. It deals with time, madness and various perceptions of what the world is or isn't. It's a study of madness and dreams, of death and rebirth, set in a world coming apart.'

Twelve Monkeys is set in a post-apocalyptic 21st-century world, but instead of a nuclear war having almost wiped out mankind, it's a killer virus that originated in 1996. Survivors live under the earth, where they are about to use a newly developed method of time travel to try and prevent the outbreak of the deadly virus.

The subject chosen for the trips back to 1990 and 1996 is James Cole (a bald headed Bruce Willis), a criminal haunted by a fragmented

Madeleine Stowe as the psychiatrist Kathryn Railly, whose credulity is stretched to the limit by Cole's story of time-travel, in *Twelve Monkeys*.

memory from his childhood. Both in 1990 and 1996, Cole meets fanatical animal rights activist Jeffrey Goines (Brad Pitt), leader of the Army of the Twelve Monkeys, who may have been responsible for the release of the virus. He also encounters a psychiatrist, Kathryn Railly (Madeleine Stowe), who finds Cole's tales of time travel and killer virus hard to believe, thinking that he's as mad as Goines. Despite this, they develop a relationship, and Cole discovers that Railly holds the key to his accomplishing his mission.

'It's a fairly complicated film,' admitted Gilliam. 'On one level it's about whether or not Cole is mad or telling the truth. The rational person is Railly, a reasonable person with a reasonable view of the world confronted by things that are inexplicable. I think what I liked most were the rantings of Jeffrey Goines. David and Janet [Peoples] were putting the kind of things that we all feel but are terrified to say into the mouth of a madman. Suddenly they became funny...'

Brad Pitt was convinced he was the right actor to play the part of crazy Jeffrey Goines. So intent was he on changing his image, he even insisted on wearing brown

Time traveller James Cole finds the past a less than restful place.

contact lenses to disguise his blue eyes, and his *Seven* buzz cut was made even scruffier.

Before he even arrived in Philadelphia for the shooting there were frenzied so-called sightings of Pitt in the city. A local Philly radio station staged 'Brad Watches' in which a host invited listeners to phone in to report any sightings of the star. Prizes were even offered for anyone who managed to break into the star's hotel room and filch something significant belonging to the actor. As far as Pitt is aware no one took up the challenge. He was only around for two weeks, but he seemed to manage to drive Philadelphia wild, with very little effort.

More work went into preparing to play his part in the film. 'He threw himself into the role,' said producer Charles Roven, ironically the husband of Dawn Steel who had headed up Columbia when Gilliam had a fracas with the studio over their botched release of *The Adventures of Baron Munchausen*. To play the manic-depressive character, Pitt spent an additional two weeks before coming to the set in group therapy sessions and he checked into a Philadelphia psychiatric ward for a day – an event that didn't get reported by the Pitt-obsessed radio station. 'He was fully in character,' said Roven of Pitt's ward visit where only the institution's director knew who the young actor was. 'He's a perfectionist.'

'Brad Pitt really wanted to do the film,' Gilliam said. 'In many ways we were lucky because he was running away from the "Sexiest Man in the world" image, so he went the other direction and he certainly won't win that award for this film. People are going to realise how funny he is. His comic timing is wonderful. It's just very, very funny stuff he's doing and he comes across as absolutely crazy.'

Continued Gilliam: 'I always like the idea of casting against type. What's interesting is that Brad has the fireworks part in the film. It's like in *The Fisher King* where Jeff Bridges is in every scene, yet Robin Williams is the one who got a lot of the credit. When Brad's on, fireworks happen. He gets all the good lines. Bruce is doing all the real hard work, and Brad gets to come in and just steal scenes. Brad is pretty laconic in some ways, then suddenly he's a blabbermouth, jabbering away at high speed. I love doing that, playing with the public's perception of that star, otherwise it wouldn't be fun.'

More fun was had by Gilliam in searching out locations. He used various places

Director Terry Gilliam (left) directs Brad Pitt and Bruce Willis in *Twelve Monkeys*.

in Philadelphia, with the Greek revival Ridgeway Library turned into the abandoned Wanamaker's Department Store, headquarters for the time-travel planning scientists in the future, and the Eastern State Penitentiary standing in for a 1990s mental hospital. Some of the film was shot in Baltimore. Much of the film has the look and feel of Gilliam's epic *Brazil*. 'I can't seem to avoid it,' admitted the director of his distinctive, steam-driven visual style.

Bruce Willis, often typecast as the action man star of the *Die Hard* movies, was as keen as Pitt to branch out into character roles. For Willis that had meant films like *Nobody's Fool* (1995) and *Four Rooms* (1995). He could understand the significance of Pitt's role in *Twelve Monkeys* to his career: 'For Brad, this is the best thing he has ever done, by far. He was just out of his mind...'

Opening at the very end of 1995 in America, *Twelve Monkeys* went straight to number one in the national box office. *Entertainment Weekly* called Pitt's Jeffrey Goines 'a jabbering psychotic who may just be more dangerous than he looks. Pitt does a hammy, bug-eyed turn, but his manic reaction time and rabid, get-a-load-of-me deviousness works for the character, and for the film's central mystery: looking at Jeffrey we can't tell where the fanatic leaves off and the put-on artist begins. Something similar might be said of Gilliam, who turns a world falling apart into a funky, dizzying spectacle.' Writer Owen Gleiberman scored the film B+.

Todd McCarthy, *Variety*'s film critic writing in *Premiere* magazine, was impressed by Pitt's off-the-wall turn in *Twelve Monkeys*: '[Cole] must endure the feverish ranting of an inmate played by Brad Pitt, whose mannered monologues and gesticulations can leave no doubt as to his sincere desire to become a serious actor.'

Becoming a serious actor was next on his career agenda, but he had more personal matters to deal with first over Christmas 1995.

Pitt was convinced from the outset that he was the
right person to play the mad Jeffrey Goines.

11 Moving Onward

JUST AS *Twelve Monkeys* opened in American cinemas, the young actor had more personal concerns on his mind. He returned home to spend Christmas with his family in Missouri, as he tried to do every year, but this time he brought Gwyneth Paltrow with him. A few days before the holidays and before departing for Missouri, Pitt decided he'd pop the question. If Gwynnie (as he affectionately called her) said 'Yes' to marriage, he'd have some really serious news to announce to his parents during the holiday visit home.

The decision had been a long time coming. Now, at the age of 32, he'd decided he was ready for marriage. There was just one problem – 23-year-old Gwyneth Paltrow wasn't. She said 'No'.

An anonymous source gave details of the failed marriage proposal to *The National Enquirer*, which ran the story at the end of January 1996. 'He thought the time was right,' said the source, 'and he just went for it. But Gwyneth didn't want to walk down the aisle just yet.' The detail of the marriage proposal suggests the tale came from a close friend of Paltrow's to whom she had confided.

Recalling his romantic antics as a schoolkid and teenager in Springfield, Missouri, Pitt had laid elaborate plans for his proposal. 'Brad got out his old picnic basket, and his favourite deli in Hollywood fixed a large pasta salad, corned beef and Swiss cheese sandwiches, New York cheesecake and tiny Christmas trees made from Reese's peanut butter candy, a bottle of wine and diet cokes.'

The source continued: 'He and Gwyneth drove to an old, romantic mansion in a secluded city park in the hills of Hollywood. They ate. Then they were just laughing and having a good time, drinking their wine, when Brad got serious. He looked at Gwyneth and quietly asked her to marry him on New Year's Eve.

'Gwyneth was stunned She looked at him for a moment, then she said, "No, not yet. Look around us, nobody in Hollywood gets married at our age and stays married. It usually doesn't last more than two years." Brad was disappointed, but he told her he understood… She explained that she was scared of commitment at that level. She told him she wanted to work hard on her career first, before they get married. She also let him know that she does not intend having children anytime soon. Brad is beginning to want kids and Gwyneth isn't ready. He may be promoted as one of the sexiest guys around, but Brad really wants to settle down.'

The picture painted of Gwyneth Paltrow's short-term personal ambitions by *The National Enquirer* were rather different to that given by the actress herself in a piece in *Interview* magazine towards the end of 1995. Her ten-year aim that September consisted of 'hopefully, I'll be married, with three or four children'. That ambition tallied with similar expressions by Pitt in *USA Today* in December, when asked where he wanted to be in his personal life in a decade's time: 'Married with bambinos and at home…'

Paltrow had strong views on marriage and had no intention of getting hitched with Pitt until she was sure he'd changed his ways when it comes to women. 'My parents have been married for 25 years and my grandparents for 55, so I take marriage and family very seriously. I wouldn't marry unless I thought it was forever.

'This last year I've been as happy as I've ever been.'

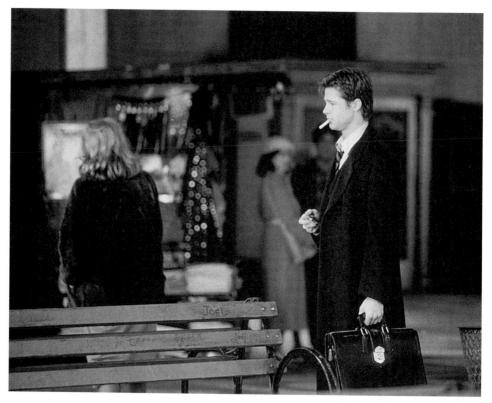

Brad on the set of Barry Levinson's *Sleepers*.

We'll have to see what happens,' she said.

Although marriage was off the agenda, their relationship was still going strong at the start of 1996, with the duo spotted house hunting in the Hamptons, an exclusive area on Long Island, a popular get-away for the rich and famous. Although people in the area were used to seeing stars and celebrities in their midst, so fearful of being spotted was Pitt that he took to wearing a yellow turban. It was a ploy he was to continue to use, hiding his face under a thick scarf and Adidas baseball cap when passing through Los Angeles International Airport in mid-January. While looking for new property to buy together, Pitt and Paltrow were staying in her Greenwich Village apartment in New York, with Pitt having all but abandoned the home at Beachwood Canyon, Los Angeles he'd bought in only 1994.

Living in New York was handy for Pitt's next film commitment. By September 1995 he'd taken the starring role in *Sleepers*, a New York-set serious drama to be directed by Barry Levinson. Levinson had enjoyed critical success with *Diner* (1982) and a series of films set in Baltimore, including *Avalon* (1990). His 'personal' movie *Toys* (1992), which had taken him years to get off the ground and starred Robin Williams, had bombed at the box office, despite being a bizarre combination of the whimsy from *Chitty Chitty Bang Bang*, *The Wizard of Oz* and *Willie Wonka and the Chocolate Factory*. With *Sleepers*, Levinson was looking to return to the mainstream of Hollywood drama.

Based on a best-selling novel by author Lorenzo Carcaterra, *Sleepers* tells the harrowing story of four street kids who murder a street vendor, only to be caught and convicted. While doing time in a juvenile jail they are sexually abused by a guard. Years later, two of the four, now grown up and back on the street, track down their tormentor and murder him. The other two are drawn into the case – one is the prosecuting attorney (played by Brad Pitt) and the other a news-hungry tabloid reporter (played by Jason Patric). The pair conspire, along with their local priest (played by Robert DeNiro), to get their old pals off. Dustin Hoffman also stars as the defence attorney.

Carcaterra had courted controversy by claiming that his novel was, in fact, non-fiction and he'd only changed names and locations to protect the identities of some of those involved. With the controversial trial of O. J. Simpson fresh in everyone's minds, the film, dealing with notions of justice, was bound to be controversial. Carcaterra had his doubts about the book, though. 'There are days when I'm sorry I wrote the book because of the physical and mental problems it has activated,' the author told a *People* magazine on-line Internet conference. 'I had to serve two functions with the writing of *Sleepers*. One was to tell my memoirs. Two was to keep identities a secret. I feel I have done that.'

Involvement alongside Barry Levinson and the stars of the movie version served to convince Carcaterra that he had indeed done the right thing, especially when he made family connections with the star. 'My daughter has become friends with Brad Pitt,' said Carcaterra. 'Since she's only 13, this has placed her as close to heaven as she's going to get.'

Pitt worked on the film for five months, wrapping the production during January 1996. 'You've never seen him so shrewd,' an on-set source said to *Entertainment Weekly*. A spokeswoman for Pitt confirmed that the actor was now choosing roles, like the part in *Sleepers*, with an eye on the future. 'He's interested in stretching. It's the roles, not the image, he's concerned with.'

Among the all-male leads on *Sleepers* was British actress Minnie Driver, who'd first come to prominence in the British TV mini-series *The Politician's Wife* (1995) before securing a small bit part role in the comeback James Bond movie *GoldenEye* (1995). 'It's kind of a weird dynamic,' she told *Premiere*, 'being the only girl.' Playing Pitt's ex-girlfriend in the drama allowed the actress a chance to get to know her co-star, but strictly on-set only. None of the *Sleepers* cast seemed particularly keen on pursuing a social life together. 'These are not people who fraternise after work. They're not the party-hearty kind of guys. If I tell any one of the boys of my female take on the situation, they kind of laugh or they go "Doh?", like Homer on *The Simpsons*.'

As Pitt and Paltrow had learned to their cost, the couple's every move had become media fodder, and Driver found herself approached by tabloid journalists asking her for the lowdown on the couple. 'Everything is prefaced by "Is it true that...?", "Is he doing this...?", and "Is she pregnant?". I'm, like, "I don't bloody know – it's a day job!".'

Despite the tabloids hovering around the Manhattan locations of the film, Pitt and Paltrow managed to get through the shooting of *Sleepers* without another media mishap on the scale of the St Barts incident.

With *Sleepers* under his belt by January 1996, but yet to be released, Brad Pitt had

Brad Pit and Paul Noonan in New York's Staten Island, the setting for part of *Devil's Own*.

a chance to enjoy the congratulations of his peers. He was stunned to discover on 22nd January 1996 that he'd won the Golden Globe award for Best Supporting Actor in *Twelve Monkeys*.

Voted on by the Hollywood Foreign Press Association, mostly elderly American journalists who write part-time for overseas publications on movies, the Golden Globes are often regarded as an accurate predictor of those stars and films likely to win Oscar nominations for the following March. Having celebrated his 32nd birthday in December (by being entertained by a troupe of lesbian strippers arranged by his singer pal Melissa Etheridge) Pitt was pleased to have his near-perfect year capped by winning a major Hollywood award.

'This last year I've been as happy as I've ever been,' he said. '[I've] been miserable, been genius, been humiliated, been congratulated, been put down – I mean the whole gamut of emotions. That's a pretty amazing year. I value that. Extremes. And it comes from acting. The hardest thing is to make it look easy.'

On the horizon there were other roles waiting. He'd contracted to star alongside Harrison Ford in *Devil's Own*, a dramatic thriller that would involve the actor in some historical and cultural research into Ireland and the history of its political troubles. In the film, Pitt plays the adopted son of Ford's Irish-American cop who

Brad receiving his Golden Globe Award for best supporting actor in
Twelve Monkeys in January 1996.

gets involved with the IRA terrorist movement. The film, directed in America and Ireland by Alan J. Pakula, acclaimed director of *Klute* (1971), *The Parallax View* (1974) and *All the President's Men* (1976) started shooting in February 1996. Rumours were soon circulating that Pitt did not get on with Ford, annoyed that the older actor was getting paid twice as much as him.

Another Irish-set film was also in contention. Pitt was reported as having expressed an interest in playing the part of IRA hunger striker Bobby Sands in a film to be directed by Jim Sheridan entitled *A Mother's Son*. His co-star would have been Helen Mirren as his mother. Sands died in May 1981 after a 66-day hunger strike and being voted in as an MP while behind bars. Sands's family objected to the whole notion of the film, though. '[It's a] naked attempt to exploit for financial gain a very painful time for us,' they said.

During a visit to Northern Ireland in December 1995 to research the part for *Devil's Own* and 'soak up the atmosphere,' according to his publicist, Pitt was spotted by a movie fan while researching Ulster's past in the Linen Hall Library in Belfast. The fan later told *The Belfast Telegraph*. 'He was happy to sign autographs, but it was clear that he didn't want it generally known that he was in town. He didn't want to be diverted from his studies in the library by celebrity-spotters.'

Staying in the Europa Hotel, Pitt booked in under the not very imaginative name of Mr Williams (William being his first given name). Staying in the hotel at the same time, and drawing more fan attention, were Manchester United footballers Ryan Giggs and Eric Cantona.

It was not all sweetness and light on the set of *Devil's Own* as production began in New York on 5th February 1996. Based on an original script by Kevin Jarre, the film is set in 1993 during the short-lived IRA ceasefire. Pitt was to play a young Irish emigré named Rory Devaney, newly arrived in New York. He's taken in by Harrison Ford's police officer Tom O'Meara. Then the cop discovers his house guest's hidden past and uncovers his bloody purpose in coming to America.

Director Alan Paluka had his hands full with two superstars on set. Harrison Ford was long used to being the main focus of his films and Pitt was fresh from his Golden Globe win and the box office success of *Seven*.

Pitt had been first on board the movie, signed by producer Larry Gordon for a reported $8 to $10 million to play the leading role of the fleeing IRA gunman. It came as a surprise to the producers of the film when Ford expressed interest in what had previously been perceived as a 'Robert Duvall-like supporting role'. More than happy with the superstar interest, Gordon quickly signed Ford up, despite his $20 million salary requirement.

The result inevitably was conflict between the two men, both of whom thought they were the leading actor, with the other in support. According to a Columbia producer, the two stars had different versions of the movie in their heads, versions in which their own character took centre stage. Soon after the February start date, Ford began tampering with the script, attempting to beef up his supporting role. An executive told *Entertainment Weekly* that Ford 'wanted his character to be showier, like Pitt's'.

Others were brought in to work on Jarre's script, including *In the Name of the Father*'s Terry George and *Lethal Weapon 3* writer Robert Kamen, as well as

Celebrating the London opening of *Legends of the Fall* with a little water.

Paluka himself. Pitt's character gained some love interest in the shape of newcomer Natasha McElhone, while some concern was expressed about 53-year-old Ford holding his own opposite the 31-year-old Sexiest Man Alive. Ford's character was made more heroic, more in line with his Han Solo, Jack Ryan and Indiana Jones personas.

Production of *Devil's Own* slowed as this additional wrangling and script work took place, pushing the budget up from almost $70 million to nearer $100 million, and the schedule reached and ran past the scheduled mid-June finish date. As the star egos continued to clash, wags on the set dubbed the film 'Star Wars'.

Recalling his role problems on *Johnny Suede* and *Legends of the Fall*, Brad Pitt took on his director and co-star head on, fighting for his own position in the film. Seeing his part dwindling as Ford's grew, Pitt held his own. After a further revision of the script by Paluka, Pitt stormed off the set, claiming the script was no longer the film he had agreed to make. However he returned to work the following day and his publicist explained the hold-up as being due to inclement weather rather than personality clashes. Ford's PR people were equally keen to play down the stories of battles on the set, dismissing 'all these ugly rumours'.

The rest of the cast and crew began to get weary as production looked like it was going to run right on into August. Actress Margaret Colin, one of the stars of the smash hit *Independence Day*, who was playing Ford's wife in *Devil's Own*, felt she'd had enough by the time July rolled around. 'The feeling is we've got to deliver a hit. I'd like to finish up now. It's too long.'

When he finally wrapped on *Devil's Own* Pitt was due to trek to Tibet to accept an $8 million offer to star in director Jean Jacques-Annaud's $50 million *Seven Days in Tibet*, which was based on a true story and which was one of two movies about the Dalai Lama mooted in 1996. Pitt was to play Austrian climber Heinrich Harrar, an Olympic gold medalist who escaped from British troops to Tibet during World War Two, ultimately becoming the Dalai Lama's tutor. The competing film, ironically, was to star Pitt's erstwhile *Devil's Own* co-star Harrison Ford in a production directed by Martin Scorsese and scripted by Ford's screenwriter wife Melissa Mathison (*ET*). Entitled *Kundun*, it was set to focus on the early life of the Dalai Lama, who was eventually forced into exile in India in 1959 a few year's after China invaded Tibet.

Pitt's project was the more likely to go into production sooner and be the first to reach the screen. However the delays on *Devil's Own* served to push the start date of *Seven Years in Tibet* back as the production waited for Pitt to become available. John Jacobs, president of worldwide marketing at the production company Mandalay, was irked by the unavailability of his star. 'We desperately want to get going,' he said in July, as Pitt and Ford battled for the soul of *Devil's Own*. 'Every time *Devil* pushes back, we have to push back. Maybe now the end is in sight for them, but no-one likes to have a movie with problems like *Devil's Own* is having.'

While Pitt was intending to live in a tent in Tibet, Gwyneth Paltrow was off to London to star alongside British actress Emma Thompson in a new adaptation of Jane Austen's *Emma*. Pitt and Paltrow made great efforts to overcome the effects of their physical separation. 'Yeah, constant separation is the worst thing for a relationship. It was a case of lots of letters to each other,' said Paltrow. 'Letters are so much better than the phone. You can always interpret things wrongly over the

On the way to a Hollywood premiere.

phone. I had never written letters in my life before. None at all.'

Whatever the fates of the competing Tibet movies, Brad Pitt will not be spoilt for choice for his future roles. From *True Romance* on he has been steadily and carefully building himself as a potential leading man, much in the image of his *Devil's Own* co-star Harrison Ford. Ford was in his mid-30s, an age Pitt was now reaching, when he hit the big time in George Lucas's 1977 space epic *Star Wars*. From his action hero beginnings as Han Solo and Indiana Jones, Ford turned himself into solid leading man material, alternating between action-based movies like *Clear and Present Danger* (1994) and light romantic comedies or drama, like Sydney Pollack's remake of *Sabrina* (1995). Pitt's future career looks set to follow a similar trajectory.

Building, perhaps, on the feel of *Legends of the Fall*, Pitt decided to take up the role of General Custer in a new version of the 1876 Little Big Horn massacre. Pitt would be following in the footsteps of actors Errol Flynn, Ronald Reagan and Robert Shaw, all of whom had played Custer at one time or another. Michael Blake, the writer of Kevin Costner's *Dances with Wolves* (1990), wrote the novel *Custer: Marching to Valhalla* which concentrated on the relationship between Custer and his wife and was to form the basis of the film.

The Golden Globe award was followed in February 1996 with an Oscar nomination for *Twelve Monkeys*, but he lost out to his *Seven* co-star Kevin Spacey, who won for his role in *The Usual Suspects*. Awards are good for bankability, but Pitt still had the urge to experiment. 'There's a fantastic, beautiful script on the life of James Dean,' he said of a proposed biopic of the young actor with whom he'd often been compared. Many other actors have also been considered for the lead role in the long gestation of this film, including Johnny Depp and Leonardo DiCaprio, and Pitt was far from convinced of his own suitability for the role. 'No way would I touch it. I'd be a fool to do it. At best, you could copy him, but there was a magic, an internal magic, that I think you would be foolish even to attempt. Everyone has such a defined image of him, from the posters, and from his films, and I think there's very few guys who have the talent to do it. I couldn't pull it off. And the other guys don't look like him, and that would disappoint the audience.'

One supporter of Pitt's taking the role is one of James Dean's contemporaries, Dennis Hopper. 'Brad Pitt has got star quality written all over him. What charisma he has! He's very versatile and has a kind of crazy compulsion to go up and down, up and down and all over – it's good and healthy to do that.'

Whether he played Dean or not, it was a testimony to his pull that he was even considered for the role. 'Brad is one of the most attractive and talented men in the world today,' thought producer David Geffen. 'He's going to be one of the biggest actors out there. He doesn't know how good he is, which is probably a good thing.'

'He's a man's man who seems to be a woman's man too,' said Nilo Otero, who was the assistant director on both *Legends of the Fall* and *Seven*. 'He's a classic American lover. He's a man that women can love and like at the same time.'

'What Brad does that you can't learn - James Dean did it really well, and [Jack] Nicholson - is that he knows how to do nothing when he's not talking,' said Jim Harrison, author of the novel that inspired *Legends of the Fall*. 'He never gives the appearance of trying to think of what to say next. So your attention is completely focused on him.'

One of Pitt's childhood friends felt that despite all the fame, glamour and attention of Hollywood, and the recognition of an Oscar nomination, Pitt hadn't changed all that much from his university days. 'All of a sudden, all of your dreams are coming true,' Bill Danziger recalled. 'It's a little overwhelming at first. That's when a person's character comes through. It's when you step back and you realise why all these people are coming on to you. If a person has it inside them, they'll still be that good person.'

Despite his rise through the ranks in Hollywood, Brad Pitt's commitment to his family and his home roots is still strong. 'I recently bought a 500-acre ranch in the Ozarks for my family,' he said. 'It's a very peaceful place. It's a feed-your-goats kind of place and I like that.' Despite outbreaks of ego on *Johnny Suede* and *Legends of the Fall* and his spats with Tom Cruise, Pitt seems to have maintained an unusual ordinariness. That is one of his attractions - the extraordinary good looks combined with a down-to-earth attitude. He doesn't fit any of the usual wild-rebel-turned-star or potenially-self-destructive-showoff tags. His nice guy act seems to be no act at all, simply his genuine personality.

Having arrived relatively easily at the top of the heap by the age of 32, it will be much harder for Brad Pitt to maintain his position, but, as always, the laid-back actor is willing to go with the flow wherever it takes him – after all, it's an attitude that has been very good to him so far.

'I believe in trusting fate,' Pitt has said. 'It's a constant. Fate always wins. Being able to choose is an even greater challenge. Back when I had to take any job I could get, it was easier. I want to do something new with every time out. Wouldn't it be great if I was in a movie and some people didn't even recognise it was me...'

Filmography

Early Work

Extra in **Less Than Zero** and **No Man's Land**

Television Series

Dallas (five episodes)
Another World

Growing Pains
'Who's Zoomin' Who?'
USA, 1987, 30 minutes
Directed by: John Tracy
Script by: Tom Walla
Production Company: Warner Brothers
Cast: Alan Thicke, Joanna Kerns, Kirk Cameron, Tracey Gold, Jeremy Miller, Lisa Capps, Rachel Jacobs, Kevin Wixted, Brad Pitt

Head of the Class
USA, 1988, 30 minutes

21 Jump Street
'Best Years of Your Life'
USA, 1988, 60 minutes
Directed by: Bill Corcoran
Script by: Jonathan Lemkin
Production Company: Patrick Hasburgh Productions in association with Stephen J. Cannell Productions
Cast: Johnny Depp, Peter DeLuise, Cheryl Pollak, H. Richard Greene, Brad Pitt, Gina Nemo, Tiffany Helm, Laura Austin

thirtysomething
'Love and Sex'
USA, 1989, 60 minutes
Directed by: Marshal Herkovitz
Script by: Liberty Hodshall
Production Companies: The Bedford Falls Co / MGM/UA
Cast: Timothy Busfield; Polly Draper; Mel Harris; Peter Horton; Melanie Mayron; Ken Olin; Patricia Wettig; David Clennon; Richard Murphy; Cheryl Pollak; Brad Pitt

Tales from the Crypt
'King of the Road'
USA, 1988, 30 minutes
Directed by: Tom Holland
Script by: J. Johnson
Based on Tales from the Crypt / Two Fisted Tales, originally published by William M. Gaines
Music by Warren Zevon
Production Company: HBO
Cast: Raymond J. Barry (Iceman); Brad Pitt (Billy); Michelle Bronson (Iceman's daughter); Jack Keller (Car dealer)

Advert: **Levi Jeans** (1988)

Films

A Stoning in Fulham County (TVM)
USA, 1988, 100 minutes
Directed by Larry Elikman
Screenplay by Jud Kinberg and Jackson Gillis
Story by Jackson Gillis
Production Company: The Landsburg Company
Cast: Ken Olin; Jill Eikenberyy; Nicholas Pryor; Ron Perlman; Theodore Bikel; Olivia Burnette; Brad Pitt; Bill Allen

Cutting Class
USA, 1989, 91 minutes
Directed by Rospo Pallenberg
Screenplay by Steve Slavkin
Production Company: April Films
Cast: Donovan Leitch; Brad Pitt; Jill Schoelen; Roddy McDowall; Martin Mull; Brenda Lynn Klemme; Mark Barnett

Happy Together
USA, 1989, 92 minutes
Directed by Mel Damski
Screenplay by Craig J. Nevius
Production Company: Metropolis Motion Pictures
Cast: Patrick Dempsey (Christopher Wooden); Helen Slater (Alexandra Page); Kevin Hardesty (Slash); Marius Weyers (Denny Dollenbacher); Barbara Babcock (Ruth Carpenter); Gloria Hayes (Luisa Dellacova); Brad Pitt (Brian); Aaron Harnick (Wally); Ron Sterling (Trevor); Eric Lumbard (Gary); Michael D. Clarke (Steve); Wendy Lee Marconi (Dory)

The Image
USA, 1989, 110 minutes
Directed by Peter Werner
Screenplay by Brian Rehak
Production Companies: HBO Pictures / Citadel Entertainment
Cast: Albert Finney (Jason Cromwell); John Mahoney (Irv Mickleson); Kathy Baker (Marcie Crawford); Swoosie Kurtz (Joanne Winslow-Darvish); Marsha Mason (Jean Cromwell); Spalding Gray (Frank Goodrich); Brad Pitt (Steve Black)

Glory Days (TV series)
Six Episodes, 50 minutes each, Fox Network, 1990
Directed by Marc Laub
Created by Patick Hapsburgh
Cast: Brad Pitt (Walker Lovejoy); Spike Alexander (Dave Rotecki); Evan Mirand (Fopiano); Nicholas Kallsen (Dominic); Beth Broderick (Sheila Jackson); Robert Costanzo (Lieutenant V.T. Krantz)

Across the Tracks (AKA Nowhere to Run)

USA, 1991, 100 minutes
Directed by Sandy Tung
Screenplay by Sandy Tung
Cast: David Belafonte (Stanford Scout); Marisa DeSimone (Salesgirl); Bebe Drake-Massey (Mrs Fischer); Annie Dylan (Linda); Thomas Mikal Ford (Coach Walsh); William Garson (Salesman); Jaime Gomez (Bobby, Teammate #1); Garon Grigsby (Thompson); John Linton (Brad); Kent Lipham (Big Ed); Chuck Lyons (Officer); Mike Marikian (Andy, Manager); Ron Marquette (Paulie, Brad's Friend #1); David Anthony Marshall (Louie); Jack McGee (Frank); Cyril O'Reilly (Coach Ryder); Brad Peterson (Stolen Car Driver); Brad Pitt (Joe Maloney); Jami Richards (Melani); Rick Schroder (Billy Maloney); Carrie Snodgress (Rosemary Maloney)

Too Young to Die?

USA, 1990, 92 minutes
Directed by Robert Markowitz
Screenplay by David Hill and George Rubino
Production Companies: Spelling / Republic Pictures / Von Zerneck-Sertner Films
Cast: Michael Tucker (Buddy Thornton); Juliette Lewis (Amanda Sue Bradley); Brad Pitt (Billy Canton); Alan Fudge (Mark Calhoun); Emily Longstreth (Jean); Laurie O'Brien (Wanda Sledge); Michael O'Keefe (Mike Medwicki)

Thelma & Louise

USA, 1991, 124 minutes
Directed by Ridley Scott
Screenplay by Callie Khouri
Production Companies: MGM/UA / Pathe Entertainment / United International Pictures
Cast: Susan Sarandon (Louise Sawyer); Geena Davis (Thelma Dickinson); Harvey Keitel (Hal Slocumb); Michael Madsen (Jimmy); Christopher McDonald (Darryl); Stephen Tobolowsky (Max); Brad Pitt (J.D.); Timothy Carhart (Harlan Puckett); Lucinda Jenney (Lena, the Waitress); Jason Beghe (State Trooper); Sonny Carl Davis (Albert); Ken Swofford (Major); Shelly Desai (East Indian Motel Clerk); Carol Mansell (Waitress); Stephen Polk (Surveillance Man)

The Favor

USA, 1991, 95 minutes
Directed by Donald Petrie
Screenplay by Josann McGibbon and Sara Parriot
Production Company: Nelson Entertainment / Shuler-Donner Productions
Cast: Harley Jane Kozak (Kathy); Elizabeth McGovern (Emily); Bill Pullman (Peter); Brad Pitt (Elliott); Larry Miller (Joe Dubin); Ken Wahl (Tom Andrews)

Johnny Suede

USA, 1992, 95 minutes
Directed by Tom DiCillo
Screenplay by Tom DiCillo
Production Companies: Miramax Films (distributor) / Vega Film Productions
Cast: Brad Pitt (Johnny Suede); Richard Boes (Man in Tuxedo); Cheryl Costa (Woman in Alley); Michael Luciano (Mr. Clepp); Calvin Levels (Deke); Nick Cave (Freak Storm); Ralph Marrero (Bartender); Wilfredo Giovanni Clark (Slick); Alison Moir (Darlette); Peter McRobbie (Flip Doubt); Ron Vawter (Winston); Dennis Parlato (Dalton); Tina Louise (Mrs. Fontaine); Michael Mulheren (Fred Business); Wayne Maugans (Ned Business); Catherine Keener (Yvonne); Joseph Barry (The Cowboy); John David Barone (Bernard); Tom Jarmusch (Conan); Samuel L. Jackson (B-Bop)

Cool World

USA, 1992, 101 minutes
Directed by Ralph Bakshi
Screenplay by Michael Grais and Mark Victor
Production Company: Morgan Creek Productions
Cast: Janni Brenn-Lowen (Mom Harris); Brad Pitt (Frank Harris); William Frankfather (Cop); Greg Collins (Cop); Gabriel Byrne (Jack Deebs); Kim Basinger (Holli Would); Michael David Lally (voice, Sparks); Michele Abrams (Jennifer Malley): Carrie Hamilton (Comic Bookstore Cashier); Stephen Worth (Comic Store Patron)

A River Runs Through It

USA, 1992, 123 minutes
Directed by Robert Redford
Screenplay by Richard Friedenberg
From the story by Norman MacLean
Production Companies: Allied Filmmakers / Columbia
Cast: Craig Sheffer (Norman Maclean); Brad Pitt (Paul Maclean); Tom Skerritt (Rev. Maclean); Brenda Blethyn (Mrs. Maclean); Emily Lloyd (Jessie Burns); Edie McClurg (Mrs. Burns); Stephen Shellen (Neal Burns); Vann Gravage (Young Paul); Nicole Burdette (Mabel); Rob Cox (Conroy); Robert Redford (narrator)

Kalifornia

USA, 1993, 118 minutes
Directed by Dominic Sena
Screenplay by Tim Metcalfe
Story by Stephen Levy
Production Company: Polygram Filmed Entertainment, in association with Viacom Pictures / Propaganda Films
Cast: Brad Pitt (Early Grayce); Catherine Larson (Teenage Girl); David Milford (Driver); David Duchovny (Brian Kessler); John Zarchen (Peter); David Rose (Eric); Michelle Forbes (Carrie Laughlin); Tommy Chappelle (Old Man); Juliette Lewis (Adele Corners); Judson Vaughn (Parole Officer)

True Romance
USA, 1993, 120 minutes
Directed by Tony Scott
Screenplay by Quentin Tarantino
Production Company: Morgan Creek Productions
Cast: Christian Slater (Clarence Worley); Patricia Arquette (Alabama Whitman); Dennis Hopper (Clifford Worley); Val Kilmer (Elvis); Gary Oldman (Drexl Spivey); Brad Pitt (Floyd); Christopher Walken (Vincenzo Coccotti); Bronson Pinchot (Elliot Blitzer); Samuel L. Jackson (Big Don); Michael Rapaport (Dick Ritchie); Saul Rubinek (Lee Donowitz); Conchata Ferrell (Mary Louise Ravencroft); James Gandolfini (Virgil); Anna Thomson (Lucy); Victor Argo (Lenny); Paul Bates (Marty); Chris Penn (Nicky Dimes); Tom Sizemore (Cody Nicholson)

Legends of the Fall
USA, 1994, 132 minutes
Directed by Edward Zwick
Screenplay by Susan Shilliday and Bill Wittliff
From the novella by Jim Harrison
Production Company: Columbia TriStar
Cast: Brad Pitt (Tristan Ludlow); Anthony Hopkins (Col. Ludlow); Aidan Quinn (Alfred); Julia Ormond (Susannah); Henry Thomas (Samuel); Karina Lombard (Isabel Two); Tantoo Cardinal (Pet); Gordon Tootoosis (One Stab); Paul Desmond (Decker); Christina Pickles (Isabel); Robert Wisden (John T. O'Banion); John Novak (James O'Banion); Kenneth Welsh (Sheriff Tynert)

Interview With the Vampire
USA, 1994, 122 minutes
Directed by Neil Jordan
Screenplay by Anne Rice (& Neil Jordan, uncredited)
From the novel by Anne Rice
Production Company: Geffen Pictures
Cast: Brad Pitt (Louis); Christian Slater (The Interviewer); Tom Cruise (Lestat); Stephen Rea (Santiago); Antonio Banderas (Armand); Kirsten Dunst (Claudia); Virginia McCollam (Whore on Waterfront); John McConnell (Gambler); Mike Seelig (Pimp); Bellina Logan (Tavern Girl); Thandie Newton (Yvette)

Seven
USA, 1995, 123 minutes
Directed by David Fincher
Screenplay by Andrew Kevin Walker
Production Company: New Line Cinema
Cast: Brad Pitt (David Mills); Morgan Freeman (William Somerset); Gwyneth Paltrow (Tracy Mills); Kevin Spacey (John Doe)

Twelve Monkeys
USA, 1995, 124 minutes
Directed by Terry Gilliam
Screenplay by David Webb Peoples and Janet Peoples
Production Companies: Atlas Entertainment / MCA / Universal Pictures
Cast: Brad Pitt (Jeffrey Goines); Madeleine Stowe (Kathryn); Bruce Willis (Cole); Christopher Plummer; David Morse

Sleepers
USA, 1996
Directed by Barry Levinson
Screenplay by Lorenzo Carcaterra and Barry Levinson
From the novel by Lorenzo Carcaterra
Production Company: Baltimore Pictures
Cast: Brad Pitt; Kevin Bacon; Robert De Niro; Minnie Driver; Dustin Hoffman; Jason Patric; Brad Renfro

Devil's Own
USA, 1996
Directed by Alan J. Pakula
Screenplay by Kevin Jarre
Production Company: Columbia Pictures
Cast: Brad Pitt (Rory Devaney); Harrison Ford (Tom O' Meara); Margaret Colin (Sheila O' Meara); Ruben Blades (Officer Edwin Diaz)

WORKS IN PROGRESS

Seven Days in Tibet
Directed by Jean Jacques-Annaud
Cast: Brad Pitt (Heinrich Harrar)

Custer: Marching to Valhalla
Screenplay by Michael Blake
Based on his novel
Cast: Brad Pitt (General Custer)